Woman In The Ancient Near East

by

Arthur Frederick Ide

Mesquite

Ide House

1982

For Further Information
write
Ide House, Inc.
4631 Harvey Drive
Mesquite, Texas 75150 U.S.A.

This is the second volume, revised and expanded edition, of the Ide House series **WOMAN IN HISTORY,** which originally appeared under the title Woman in the Civilization of the Ancient Near East.

Library of Congress Cataloging in Publication Data

Ide, Arthur Frederick.
   Woman in the ancient Near East.

   (Woman in history ; 2)
   Rev. ed. of: Woman in the civilization of the ancient Near
East. c1981.
   Includes bibliographical references.
   1. Women—Near East—History. 2. Civilization, Ancient.
I. Title.   II. Series.
HQ1726.5.I3   1982   305.4'09394   81-24195
ISBN 0-86663-069-4

For
CHARLES ANTHONY STANLEY IDE
and
PROFESSOR JOHN L. EIKLOR
UNIVERSITY OF NORTHERN IOWA

Jericho & Sumeria

Exactly when and where civilization began in the ancient Near East remains a point of speculation among contemporary historians. Most texts argue that civilization began in Mesopotamia: the Greek name for the land between the Tigris and Euphrates rivers that have their headwaters in the mountains of Armenia in modern Turkey. Mesopotamia has been given this honor because of the existence of the city of Jericho; which has been described by the Greek author Xenophon, who wrote in the year 401 B.C.: "In this area the land is a level plain just like the sea, full of wormwood. If there was any brush or reed there, it was invariably fragrant, like the spices."[1].

Just above the Dead Sea in Palestine, Jericho was fashioned around the year 8000 B.C.. The original city lasted approximately 1000 years before it was destroyed by various calamities. It's history is brief, as very little of its past was recorded. At best the historian-archaeologist can argue that its embryonic society was one composed of food gatherers, a few hunters, and even less traders or merchants. The majority of its people were women: the men died off early in life, spent in war or intrasocietal fightings which were seen as sport. The women tilled the small gardens, and for the most part brought in the root crops that were diligently and painfully cultivated: water had to be carried in by any means (traditionally by being drug up from wadis in earthen vessels which soon disintegrated under the moisture of their contents). Naked children were usually with them, for the men stayed at home within the city preparing for war or sport.

Women in the earliest days of the first Jericho probably enjoyed more rights than their granddaughters, for the early society needed the united support of all to survive. But this was to change.

The second city of Jericho appeared shortly after the collapse of the first. It was, in fact, built upon the ruins of the old city. It achieved even greater fame, being surrounded by a stout stone wall several feet thick which sported a large omnibus tower that gave witness not only to the city's watchfulness but also its growing concern of being invaded.

The houses in the second Jericho were made out of sun-dried bricks which were fashioned by hand. The homes were neither spacious nor lavishly built. Their floors were pacted clay overwhich straw was laid. The rooms had soaring ceilings for the houses enjoyed doomed roofs similar to today.

The furniture in the home of the residents of early Jericho can only be described as primitive. The vast majority were constructed out of wood in slab form. These pieces were primarily a bench or two, a plank table of narrow width to lay food on or to knead bread, and a small shelf on which to raise a deity. Later, in Jericho social history, a rudimentary cupboard appeared, being the skeletal outline of a contemporary cupboard, fashioned out of four joined planks of wood. Then, as the first millennia drew near the foundations of bed structures probably generated, and with them came the employment of fabrics, basically homespun flax, into covers and coverlets. The very poor, however, would not enjoy this innovation and luxury until the end of the age. Instead they had at best a rock on which to lay their head, eating their meals and conversing sitting on the ground. A cloth which served as a rug was a rare fortune, and undoubtedly only used during periods of social intercourse.

Social intercourse usually followed a celebration consuming foods which were prepared outdoors. The majority of the diet centered around root crops and cereals which were mixed together into a vegetable oil or animal fat, sprinkled with almonds and pistachios, and fried until brown. Supplemental foods included peas, apples, and hackberries. The hackberry was especially popular, being squashed into a fermented drink that made the other world of spirits seem much closer when consumed.

While the men primarily gathered the grain and labored it into flour, it was the women of ancient Jericho who tended the herds, drew the milk (especially from the sheep) to make yogurt and cheese, and on special occasions slaughtered an animal to plenish the larder. Women also were the bee-keepers, for the people of Jericho were especially fond of honey which was used as their only sweetner. The trove of hives however was small, and so many a Jericho woman counted her wealth and importance by the number of hives she maintained, and the quanitity of their produce. Men seldom interferred with this industry.

If the honey harvest was good, women were eager to spend what surplus could be afforded for individual luxuries, such as securing stones, sea-shells, and jewels to fashion into collars, belts, nose-rings, and rings. Women's jewelry was generally light in weight and smaller in proportion than the jewelry that adorned the naked bosoms of men in ancient Jericho.

The men of ancient Jericho delighted in larger and more heavy stones and jewels. They saw their collars and belts as talismans of their masculinity.

Jewelry had a religious as well as a social significance for the early inhabitants of Jericho. It was worn during all social meetings. If the meeting was of a somber or more serious nature it was kept in low profile or not worn at all; but, if the meeting was to jubilate over a military victory or bountiful harvest, it was worn lavishly

and conspicuously. More somber occasions concerned death. Women in ancient Jericho were quick to
become criers of some renown. Not only did they
leave their jewels at home, but painted their
breasts, foreheads, palms, and feet with a mixture
of ashes and mud. At the internment of the cadaver they beat their breasts lamenting the passing of the deceased, sobbingly ejaculated that
they would trade even their great jeweled collars
for the deceased's return. If this prayer was powerful and moved the kindred of the dead they were
paid either a coin or another jewel. Some women,
who were especially dramatic in mourning the passing of the dead, became quite wealthy as testified
by the number of coins on the collars they were
buried with.

Worship services for the deities were the
opposite of burials. During these services women
brought out their most elaborate jewels, and tried
even to secure large jewels and sea shells in
their hair.

Most of this primitive worship service was
without liturgy or fanfare. Generally it was an
individual family matter, and the actual act of
worship was generated in the family home. The worship itself was woman-oriented for the primary deity was a goddess who transmorgified into three separate stages: from being very young and beautiful,
to being a mother in childlabor, to changing into
a very old and withered woman who was recognized
as a sage of time. As a young woman the goddess
gave promise to abundance, such as the planting of
crops, the mating of animals, and the sexual at-
traction between individuals. This came to frui-
tion when she gave birth to a child (which was usually a girl), thereby continuing the promise for
abundance, productivity, and regeneration; along
with this stage was the acknowledgement of crop
cultivation and harvesting. The old woman was a
promise of sustaining life, of maturing, and of

wisdom: a prophecy, in fact, of social recognition that elderly individuals would be around and should not be discarded. The old woman was the winter of theology: within her withered breasts lay memories of the past and understanding that she would be succeeded by other women.

Regeneration was critical in the thinking of ancient Jericho, for if there was no promise of new generations the entirety of the community was threatened. Thus the productivity of the woman was essential to the well being of the community. For this reason the goddess was paramount, and her worship service and its location was central.

The tabernacle of the goddess was in a central room, or in the center of a single room. If the house was large the central room was linked by the spokes of other rooms. If the home owner was wealthy there could be several such rooms or the image of the goddess was repeated and placed in adjoining rooms in miniature form.

Along with the fertility goddess were the images of bulls and rams. Their phallic representation was again to insure fecundity, and their likenesses were either painted on the walls directly or modeled and molded in plaster to be set on the walls and shelves. Then too it was not infrequent for the horns of slain animals to be set erect in benches to heighten the drama.

In the more affluent homes there was even a room set aside for the care of the dead. Not only did it have the customary markings of the other rooms, especially the embellished likenesses of the goddess and her animals, but additionally there were frescoes of the dead in various states of dying and decomposition. Included in this macabre art were the gruesome tales of the inevitable: the cadavers being chewed apart by vultures who did not rest until the corpse was headless. In this instance women were definitely equal to men for the vultures played no favorites.

Decomposition, however, was not played by chance, nor left either to the passage of time or the carniverous appetites of birds. Instead it was generally the custom to strip the body of its flesh, and then wrap it in cloth. After it had been left exposed to the night air in this attire, it was finally buried, usually beneath the main floor. Only rarely was the cadaver removed to a different location. In such cases it was picked up by professional mourners who came at the front of carts dragged by donkeys, cows, goats, or occasionally a yoke of oxen. Wheels were not yet available.

Oxen were a blessing to transportation needs, appearing around 3000 B.C. in domestic use. Their purpose, however, was for many things, including dragging the newly invented plow across parched ground that would be washed by a primitive irrigation. Their employment brought more acres under cultivation, and in turn increased the city's prosperity. As her prosperity increased so too did her zest for living and desire for new goods.

The women quickly bartered their surplus for new goods, especially those goods which increased and gave new flavor to their diet. However, instead of securing perishables, except on a limited scale, they bartered for seeds and vines, especially the grape vine, which were set out, water brought in, and the fruit watched over.

While the women worked at caring for the grape, the men talked and fought among themselves, or prepared for war. The men, however, became interested when it was discovered that the grape pressed made an exhilerating beverage that seemed to have the power to raise the consciousness of the inbiber to the throned world of the celestial deities. They lost their adversion to work and were in the front, making vats and barefootedly pressing the grape into wine. But soon it became obvious that the wine made required larger vessels to store it in the pots Jericho society fashioned. Soon the potter turned out larger vessels, and in time began to decorate them. As their strength and endurability increased, so too did its ornamentation: from geometric designs to pictographic histories. With the development of pottery a new industry was also born. With it came the need for some means of record of the transaction and business of the Sumerian society.

To account for the harvest and other productions (and, too, to regulate the life and action of various citizens) writing came into its own. By 3000 B.C., the Sumerians had devised a system of writing known as cuneiform which was quickly adopted also by the Akkadians, Assyrians, Babylonians, and Persians. This invention came with the development of wedge-shaped tools which were pressed into wet clay to create pictures which stood for words. The very nature of this writing presented definite limitations (according to modern thinking), as cuneiformic writing is unable to represent abstract ideas and relationships. This however was not considered of significance to Sumerians, for such ideas seldom occupied their attention; they were far more concerned with the immediate needs of their time.

These needs have been preserved in the tablets they left behind. Among the records we have today, we know that slavery existed in ancient Sumeria. It was a recognized institution that had quasi-devine sanction.

The majority of the slaves in ancient Sumeria were women. Generally they were brought to the market, having been captured in the mountains. They had been selected for their large, sturdy frames, for their fortitude,Part of these legends included tales of witches, witchery, and witch-craft.

Witches were devils who took on the form of women. They entered the hostess' body through her vagina or mammery nipples. Occasionally the satanic force would enter through a new orifice (or vent) which was covered over by a patch of brown darkened skin, such as a mole. Once the mephastophelian force had entered the woman it would make her crazed with passion, and in quest to sustain herself she would seek out victims whom she would arouse with her tongue either in speech given to gossip (to create either jealousy or anger), or by physically caressing the victim's erogenous zones so that s/he would become powerless to escape the evil will. Sex was a major part of this, and thus sex was to be strictly regulated, for it was believed that overstimulation and sexual excitement could lead to the downfall of a nation, and this was considered the ultimate result of witchcraft.

Since witchcraft and witches were equally unforgivable, anyone who was accused of witchcraft and practicing the dark art, or even simply labeled a witch or warlock (the male witch), were made to undergo a trial by ordeal. If they passed they were allowed to live but expelled from the community, for the common belief held that if such an accusation did occur, even if it was not proven, there had to be some fact to generate the accusation. If the accused did not and could not pass the trial by ordeal, death was the penalty, and the accused was dispatched with haste.

The trial of witches and warlocks was unique. The accused was taken before the shrine of the local deity (usually a goddess), had the charge read (or repeated, since the accuser did not always have to be present at the trial), and then bound. Once bound the accused was taken to the river (such as the Euphrates) and thrown into the water. It was believed that once this action had occurred the deity would decide the guilt or innocent of the accused. The decision of the deity was read in the results of the action. If the accused sank, s/he was declared innocent for the holy waters accepted her/him as one of their own. However, if the accused floated superstitious Sumerians summized concluded that the water was rejecting an imperfect being who was unholy. Thus one who floated, either because of knowledge on how to keep one's breath, or basic bouyancy condemned his/herself. The difficulty with witchcraft and being a witch or a warlock was the fact that the reality or accusation of the same damned one's entire family. Not only did the witch/The popular way of stopping witches and witchery was to make the home all important so that the woman would not consider leaving. The homes were not much, by contemporary standards, but still time was invested to see to it that a few rudimentary comforts were brought in, and the woman was given increased dominion and authority over the house and its possessions, management, and direction. In the area of witchcraft and warlockry, the accused not only condemned his/herself, but too his/her spouse, children, and kindred. So great was the social fear (or misunderstanding) of the reputed ocult art that any nearness to it or semblance of it was enough to set society to paniced fevered pitch with an intensity so strong that homes would be broken into, suspects dragged out, and summary trial clandestinely held. The fear was generated by the belief that witches were thrown upon the society by their enemies: individuals, tribes or nations which wished to suppress them, destroy them, or enslave them. This paranoia was so intense that at times some witches were walled up behind massive sets of stone, or crushed beneath tabled rocks.

Another objection to witches and witchery was the belief that witches were participants in "un-natural" sexual acts, ranging from copulation with incubus and/or succubus (the incubus was generally a male demon that had sexual relations with women, while the succubus was the female demon that had sexual relations with the male) which would lead to homosexual activities and the surrender of the "purpose" for sex: the procreation of additional laborers and warriors to maintain the freedom and prosperity of the society. Homosexuality was especially denounced since it was believed that this sexual expression was of such abandonment and pleasure seeking that the rigid familial orientation would be deminished if it was allowed basic freedom. To this end homosexuals, both men and women, were put to death on the charge of treason against the state and against the home or family. Seldom was an accused homosexual pardoned, and never was one found innocent of the accusation.

The act of union with demons supposedly also occurred late at night, when it was the darkest. Reputedly those women which were trapped by the fatal charms of the incubi/succubi, were spirited out of their homes by a mighty wind to a distant grove where a purgatorial fire burned with hellish ferocity. Then with total disregard for the sexual traditions and moralities learned, the neophytes seeped themselves into a wild orgy. This had to be stopped.

As the fevor against witches and witchcraft grew, men began to imprison their wives in the home. Bound by this, women, in an attempt to give themselves an identity and to make the house more livable, began to concentrate on interior design and decoration, although only in a most rudimentary nonscientific sense. While the design and accessorization of the dwellings of the majority of the people aren't clear due to the absence of any real documentary evidence, vivid descriptions remain of palaces treated with colored tiles crested with motifs and emblems of surrealistic designs. Furthermore art work decorated walls and floors which were made with precious and semiprecious stones, exotic woods, alabaster, onyx, lapis lazuli, agates, and even gold. These homes were filled with art. The

most common art work was nature oriented. Murals
and frescoes depicted numerous animals who grazed,
were ridden, pulled plows and carts, procreated,
and relieved their bodily needs. In addition they
are pictured with heroes and gods. The gods are
the tallest figures, and are presented stiffly, al-
most lifeless. Heroes have a little more ambi-
tion, and are neither staid nor ossified. Frequently the heroes are depicted engaged killing
lions and other wild beasts. Heroines, on the
other hand, are illustrated saving captives, cele-
brating worship, and caring for children.

The only civilizations which rivaled Sumeria
in the Near East were Babylon and Chaldea. Egypt
rivaled and surpassed it in the south.

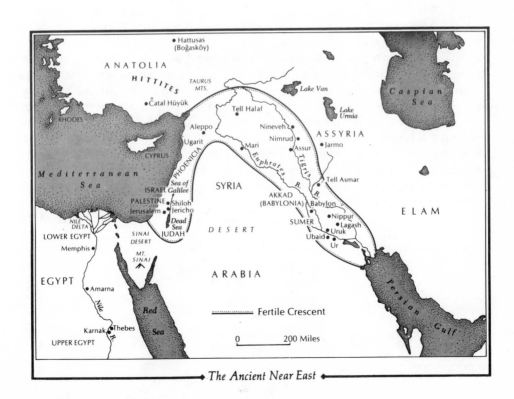

◆ *The Ancient Near East* ◆

There are few records of Chaldean society. It was a brief but prosperous society which dates from approximately 4000 B.C.. These people were industrious, and built magnificent buildings out of sun-dried bricks. Over these bricks they placed delicately carved, translucent alabaster and bas-relief. Inside their buildings, unlike the Sumerians, they enjoyed a special refinement: hanging across their walls rich and magnificent fabrics and tapestries. These wall cloths contained the images of legendary tales and heroic events. No subject was taboo for depiction and illustration. Instead the age revelled in being able to portray every slice of life in its entirety. Women did not have a major role in Chaldean society. They were, for the most part, passive and unassuming. The man controlled the situation and the life style. The woman followed his will and his body, usually walking behind him, and with a bowed head.

The majority of the woman's time was occupied by basic domestic tasks. Cooking a hearty meal for the man was foremost. These meals were primarily grain meals; meat was scarce and difficult to cook over the low fires which were maintained in primitive ovens set into pits in the center of the home's main room. Their records are similar to those of ancient Babylon. Thus the best picture we can get will come with a study of ancient Babylon.

Mesopotamia

Babylon

There are more records of man's attitude toward women in ancient Babylon than elsewhere at the same time. Not only do we have records detailing male attitude toward women, but also a rather extensive legal code on the rights of women.

Women enjoyed more protection and freedom in Babylon than they did in Chaldean society, but this was the case only as long as their life revolved around the home and the family.

Most of the laws dealing with women in ancient Babylon were centered around the institution and social conditions that were presumed to insure the perpetuation and prosperity of the family, for woman's greatest function, it was believed, was to give birth "to generations without end." Still this injunction must not be

The Gugurri Gate, Assur
Assur, the first capital of the Assyrians, was founded as a fortress commanding the upper valley of the Tigris river. Etching from Walter Andrae, *Das Wiedererstandene Assur* (Leipzig: J. C. Hinrichs Verlag, 1938), p. 6

seen as a license to promiscuity and sexual abandonment. Ancient Babylon was anything but a liberal society, and monogamous fidelity was the rule. Monogamous fidelity, however, did not have to include the concept or ability to love. And, monogamous fidelity was maintained only after a formal marriage had been contracted.

Marriage in ancient Babylon was a business arrangement. It was determined by the fathers of the future bride and groom even before either of the children had been born. Only the final arrangements were made with the imput of the future groom when the boy-child was considered to have reached the age of reason.

Having achieved puberty, and successfully having proved his ability to generate "the white blood" to insure the perpetuation of his family line, the prospective groom met with the father of the future bride to complete the arrangements made earlier. He presented the father of the bride a gift of money, prototype to the dowry. If the gift was acceptable, the father of the bride consented. The acceptability of the gift was determined on the basis of its size and value, and once it was accepted the father of the future bride provided his daughter with an inheritance which she would retain ownership over even after her marriage had been consummated. (Although the bride retained ownership over the parental gift, the future husband administered it for her and enjoyed any immediate profit it brought, while acknowledging publicly the significance and meaning of the gift.) Her inheritance was a statement protecting her rights and status, for now she too had maintenance, and would enjoy a near equality in the area of finances as would her future husband.

If, for any number of reasons, she was not given this gift by her father the marriage would not occur, for the contract would not have been fulfilled. The law read specifically, on this matter:

> If a man has taken a wife and has not executed the marriage contract, that woman is not a wife.[2]

Marriage was not considered espeically sacred, at least in line with contemporary Judaic-Christian standards. It was for convenience and to perpetuate the nation. It could be dissolved by either party as long as the person who dissolved it was able to pay the penalty required by the jurist, or to pay a stiff fine if a cash settlement was sought. If the marriage was able to last it did so for reasons of security. For marriage to last meant that at least the wife accepted rigid and confining standards. Paramount among these standards was the legislated requirement that she was sexually monogamous. Any sexual act that occurred outside of marriage or without her husband participating was strictly forbidden.

Adultery was the most grevious infraction of the rule demanding sexual fidelity and monogamy. The penalty for adultery was death:

> If a man's wife be caught lying with another, they shall be strangled and cast into the water...[3]

The strange thing about this injunction was that it applied only to women. Furthermore it was the responsibility of the woman to prove herself innocent at all times. A man could accuse his wife of adultery even if he had not caught her in the act. In such a case the wife could clear herself only with a compurgation: calling in witnesses to testify to the gods that she spoke the truth, afterwhich she would call on the gods to confirm her words that she was innocent. As long as a bolt of lightening did not strike her dead immediately, she was declared innocent.

Still she had no way of undoing the false accusation or suspicion and her husband suffered no penalty for his calumny.

There was a greater danger, however, than just a jealous husband's accusation and suspicion. This danger lay in the jealousy or spite of any man who would publily accuse her of adultery:

If a man's wife has the finger pointed at her on account of another, but has not been caught lying with him, for her husband's sake she shall plunge into the sacred river[4]

She was only adjudged innocent if and when she could float after she had been thrown into the water with her hands tied tightly behind her back. (Pity the poor woman who could not swim nor hold her breath!) If she floated, or swam back to shore she was afforded some satisfaction. Her accuser was publicly humiliated by having half of his hair and beard shaved off. (In this regard it is interesting to note that the law acknowledges the accuser to suffer this penalty to be men, which is an indication that most of the accusations came from men, for their is no reference as to what a woman who was an accuser should suffer if the accused returned alive to shore). At the same time the accused was allowed to return to her husband's home with no jeopardy or penalty.

The only difference in this was that while the woman was expected to remain monogamously faithful, there was no injuction for the man to be the same. In fact the man was seldom faithful or monogamous. A man could have sex with any woman he found interest in. He was allowed to have children by a slave woman and raise the slave's offspring in his house, requiring his wife to treat his bastards as if they were legitimate and her own. In fact, the philandering husband could legalize the bastards by publicly recognizing them as his own; by doing so he inherited them and made them equal to any legitimate heirs born to his original marriage:

If a man has had children borne to him by his wife, and also by a maid, if the father in his lifetime has said, "My sons," to the children whom his maid bore him, and has reckoned them with the sons of his wife; then after the father has gone to his fate, the children of his wife and of the maid shall share equally. The children of the wife shall apportion the shares, and make their own selections.[5]

If the father of the bastards failed to recognize them while he was still alive, the maid or slave and her children were emmancipated upon his death. Their emmancipation worked to lessen the inheritance of the legitimate heirs since they were a part of that inheritance. This sometimes led to fratricide by either the legitimate or illegitimate descendents.

When the legal wife suspected her husband of adultery (or caught him in the act of adultery) she had no legal recourse. She was expected to accept the situation or remove herself from the man's house. Divorce was difficult at best since any wife bringing a letter of divorce to a judge was required to prove that she was without vice and had never committed any social indiscretion:[6]
If a woman has hated her husband, and has said, "You shall not possess me," her past shall be inquired into, as to what she lacks. If she has been discreet, and has no vice, and her husband has gone out [on her], and has greatly belittled her, that woman has no blame, she shall take her marriage portion and go off to her father's house

18

[But, if she was found to be "indiscreet," and] has gone out, has ruined her house, and has belittled her husband, she shall be drowned[7]

The principle was sexual in scope and nature. While the woman was to be chaste, the man was not, and was able to obtain a divorce with no great difficulty, provided he give his wife the equivalent of her marriage price and returned her dowry. The purpose of such divorces enabled the man to marry again and produce other children to carry on his name. Indirectly the law had a two-fold reasoning: it unshakled the man from a barren wife which was at that time quite pyschologically unsettling since fecundity was a hallmark of manhood and strength, and at the same time it provided the released woman a means of support.

Divorce was also easier for the man to obtain if there had been any difficulties within the existing marriage, especially if those difficulties revolved around "socially unacceptable practices or experiences". A woman was considered a social deviant if she burned her husband's bread or pottage, was a spend-thrift, or belittled her husband in public. If any of these reasons were presented to the judge the verdict ruled not only in the favor of the plantiff (the man), but also freed the man from any future or further obligations:[8]

If a man's wife, living in her husband's house, has persisted in going out, has acted the fool, has wasted the house, has belittled her husband, he shall prosecute her. If her husband has said, "I divorce her," she shall go her way; he shall give her nothing as her price of divorce. If her husband has said "I will not divorce her," he may take another woman to wife; [and the first] wife shall live as a slave in her husband's house.

Babylonian law also indirectly protected women if they were invalids, or suffering from a critical or terminal illness, from being put out of her house.[9] Furthermore it required the husband to maintain such a woman as long as she lived without creating social discord or antipathy. In that Babylon was far more generous than later societies.

There was only one serious social crime that could be committed by the invalid wife that could cost her her support and even her life: to be discovered gossiping. Gossiping distressed Hammurabi, and led to a plethora of laws to end gossiping: if any woman was found to be a gossip she was to be immediately and unceremoniously drowned.[10]

To keep women from gossiping men curtailed women's basic civil rights. To keep her from complaining, husbands were encouraged to keep their wives pregnant. If she gave birth to a girl she was to try again, and in the interrum see to it that the girl dutifully learn all domestic duties necessary to keep a man happy, and as the child grew she was to represent the father without showing any independence of thought or character.

The man was absolute and supreme; he could determine destiny, composition, and final reward for all things. If the father disliked a son he could disinherit him; and, if the son had committed some "grave misdemeanor" (such as lying, stealing from the family larder, or engaging in any homosexual act) the father could have the boy sold into slavery. Girls were treated in a similar manner, except if the girl should engage in any lesbian activity she could be put to death.[11]

The Babylonian objection to homosexuality was not passed on any religious belief, but rather concern about the continued propoagation of the society. Homosexuals usually did not have children, and adults who did not have children were viewed as traitors to the state. Treason was punishable by death.[12]

Since the father was absolute in authority
and control he was seldom opposed. Sons and
daughters obeyed him out of fear, far more so than
out of love or respect. If either the son or the
daughter disobeyed their father they could be
drowned; if either attempted to physically strike
out against his/her father, the assailant's hand
would be cut off. But even under such a
threat there were rebellions, although few were
ever successful.[13]

Daughters had the most difficult life of Babylonian children. They were made totally depend-
ent upon the will and whim of their father.
Little succor could be gained by turning to their
mother who had no authority to approve, reprove,
or condone or condemn any wish or act that they
would make. Fathers had little concern about or
for their daughters. They were the ones who mourn-
ed the loudest when girls were born, and the first
whose tears dried when she died.

The daughter's destiny was determined from
birth by the father. The majority of the girls
born into Babylonian civilization were scheduled
for a domestic life, married, encumbered by numerous children, filled with hard work and a short
life, only to be replaced by a younger woman when
they either died or were divorced. A few girls
were more fortunate. Their fathers scheduled them
for the life of a religious votary.

Respected and sought out (since they communi-
cated directly with the deities supplicating for
peace, prosperity and fecundity for all of the
people of Babylon) extra care was spent on their
comfort and life. Numerous laws were enacted to
preserve the special nature and function of the
religious votary. She was legislated to be a per-
petual virgin (unless she was sought out by a god

who wished to give to the earth a special half-god/half-human being in testimony of his divine love for Babylon; frequently when this was the case the god chose the body of the temple priest to express his affection to the people through the votary).

She was not to frequent disreputable places, especially those shops which sold beer.[14] Beer was a man's drink. It was considered unseemly for a woman to be seen drinking it. The objection to a religious votary entering (much less alone patron-izing) a beer shop was based on the common concen-sus that "seditious slanderers" frequented such establishments and could injure the votary's ears which were tuned to the messages of the divini-ties. Furthermore, it was feared, that these same "seditious slanderers" would tempt her from her comittment to the religious life, her vow of chast-ity, her singularity of purpose, and her devotion to public assistance. Beer was a drug.[15]

The majority of the "seditious slanderers" were foreigners who plotted the overthrow of the state, while a few of the most "unsavory" individuals who were labeled "unpatriotic citizens" "joined in the sedition."

If a votary did enter such a place as a beer shop she was initially reprimanded by the priest. A second infraction would bring a verbal chastisement from the secular authorities. A third such occurance would demand that the votary's father come to get her and take her from the temple to the mutual shame of both. If it occurred after that, the ex-votary was put to death. Such was the penalty for drinking beer. The law was clear:[16]

If a votary, who is not living in the

convent, open a beer-shop for drink, that woman shall be put to death.

If "seditious slanderers" were found near her, they were punished severly, but not executed. If a bar maid or the owner was present and served the votary in any capacity, "that beer-seller shall be put to death."

By the days of Hammurabi several women dedicated to religion sought to publicly practice their faith, moreso than merely testifying to it. They became "sisters of the street": taking their apostleship to the masses on an intimate and direct basis. Since they worked, ate, and lived with the poor the law expected them to be especially pure and holy with no earthy overtones to their person or character. They were to be the paramount examples of purity; any infringement on their purpose and image was considered to be an act of treason and thus deserving of death.

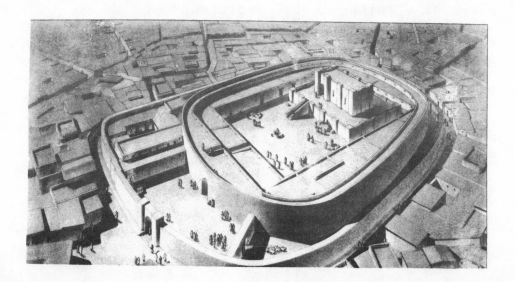

Occasionally a votary married. To preserve her public image she was required to take a vow of chastity. If her husband grew restless because she had chosen the life of a celebate, he could take a concubine (never a mistress) "and work his will upon her". (The votary, at times, even helped in the selection of the concubine.) The concubine was selected and married quickly to provide the man with heirs. Both women lived under the same roof, yet eventhough the concubine lived with the man and the votary she was never permitted to consider herself an equal.[17] At best she was a surrogate wife with no rights or freedoms. Her sole responsibility was to give the husband heirs.

In many ways she was treated and seen as either as a slave or servant. There was some degree of equality, however, in such marriages, in regard to debts and the extension of debts. Long before it became a facet in the legal process of other societies, Babylonian civilization recognized community property: both in real estate, and in the area of debts and obligations. The law read:

From the time that that woman [a wife] entered into the man's house they shall be liable for all debts subsequently incurred.[18]

This joint responsibility only applied to debts contracted after the marriage had taken place. Debts contracted before marriage were strictly the responsibility of the individual who acquired the indebtedness. If either incurred debt before the marriage, the party which incurred the debt was required by law to pay that debt off by his/herself:

...if that man had a debt upon him before he married that woman, his creditor, shall not take his wife for it. Also, if that woman had a debt upon her before she entered that man's house, her creditor shall not take her husband for it.[19] [The wife could escape the legal obligation to pay off any of her husband's debt after marriage if he granted her a signed writ exempting her from any such legal obligations]: If a woman, living in a man's has persuaded her husband to bind himself, and grant her a deed to that effect that she shall not be held for any debt by a creditor of her husband[20]

Babylonian women had the right to be protected from the physical abuse of their husbands. If she was hit, scorned, publicly humiliated or repudiated she could return to the home of her father. Once she had returned home it was her father's responsibility to attempt to correct the situation and reconcile the estranged couple. If the difficulty could not be corrected, or if both of the parties preferred a divorce, the wife was allowed to recover her dowry, and given custody of any of the children she had had by the man. Babylon was the only civilization at this time, and for centuries later, that believed that a woman was the best qualified to raise the young. Seldom, if ever, was the man given custody of the young. This was the case not because the court believed that the father was incapable of raising the young, but because the woman was considered to be more capable than the man who, the courts reasoned, should be free to "pursue manly goals of war and chance."

Women in Babylon were also permitted to engage in business. Few professions or occupations were closed to Babylonian women, although not all avenues of commercial adventure were open to women who were not Babylonian by birth.

Babylonian women engaged in some form of business or industry were granted the same rights, privileges, and responsibilities as enjoyed by male businesspersons. If the woman contracted a debt in regard to her business she was expected to pay it off without seeking any recourse from her husband or the state. This remained the situation until Babylon fell in 1170 B.C., to the Kassite hordes who emigrated from present-day Iran. These strange and barbaric people, fleeing an unhappy land which endured regular famines and bad harvests, came to Babylon in quest of homes, workers, and food, determined to obtain their goals regardless of cost. The individual was expendable for the good of the tribe.

Cuneiform Tablet, Assur
The clay tablet records the sale of a female slave named Likanu. Lowie Museum of Anthropology, University of California, Berkeley

Standard of Ur
depicts farm life, the market, and feasting.
Courtesy of the Trustees of
the British Museum

Kassite Interlude

Kassite women had no rights at all. They were considered mere appendages of men; they survived at the pleasure of their men who were unchecked in any way. These ultra-conservative, ultra-reactionary people afflicted every civilization that they came in contact with, giving Babylon an uncreative rule for five hundred years. No new construction appeared. No noticable advance in any of the arts, nor in religion, nor in philosophy occured.

It was truly a dark age Babylon suffered. A conquered people they secretly prayed for their own liberation while building cavernous treasuries out of unsecured stone which fell on top of the fearfull as earthquakes moved large sections of the earth; yet there was no complaint for it seemed to be a gentler death than the living hell experienced under the Kassites.

The bloodthirsty inhumanities perpetrated by the Kassites were not squelched until the advent of the Assyrians who came from western Asia, ultimately settling around the city of Nineveh.

Assyria to New Babylon

The Assyrians were a Semetic people. They had for a long time resided to the north of Babylon, assimilated some of the Babylonian culture, but with a temporary subjection to the tyranny of the Kassites, they developed a military culture in order to survive. In many ways they were similar to Sparta.

Women did not fare well under Assyrian rule, either as Assyrians, or as women captured, enslaved, or subjected to the conquest of Assyria. The Assyrians universally adopted a policy of extreme harshness because of their own memory of the extraordinary pain they had experienced under the Kassites. Even still the ill-treatment Assyrians visited upon those people they conquered was far less severe than the tortures twisted under Kassite rule; yet, Assyrian brutality was so henious that when the Assyria collapsed in 612 BC, the Hebrew prophet Nahum celebrated its demise in one of the most poignant books of the Bible, while lamenting the rise of their conquerors: the New Babylonians (who history records as the Chaldeans), who gave history the legendary gardens, and the account of Queen Esther the Jew.

The New Babylonians were more powerful than the old. They extended their empire throughout the fertile crescent.[21]

New Babylon was supported by trade, not warfare. Commerce was supreme and the businessman came to the front of society. No longer did the warrior monopolize the attention of chroniclers and poets, instead it recorded the most famous ruler of New Babylon was King Nebuchadnezzar II (604-562 B.C.) who not only rebuilt the city of Babylon, but ushered in a redolent renaissance in architecture, art literature, and science which was grounded firmly on the strength of Babylon's economic prosperity. (Although extreme attention was paid to astrology, new insights and discoveries occured in astronomy. Several planets were discovered, and the sky was divided into twelve equal parts and denoted with one distinct and separate sign of the zodiac.)

The capital city was rebuilt to become the legendary **el dorado** of towers and hanging gardens. Entrance into this metropolis was by way of a forty-foot high Ishtar Gate that spanned the Processional Way where the revered god Marduk was carried on the bare backs of sweating men at the climax of the New Year festival. The city itself gave shelter to more than 250,000 people who lived in homes sprawled across 500 acres, surrounded by brightly painted brick walls that were so wide that chariots could pass along its top. The famed Procession Way itself was a marvel. It was 63 feet wide and made of red and white stone. At its end was the awesome ziggurate: seven stories tall, rising from a base 300 feet wide, where both men and women worshipped (although men served as the chief officiants).[22]

Mesopotamian deities and humans were basically equal.[23] The gods lived and worked as did Mesopotamian individuals; each had his or her own separate task, station in life, and concern.[24] The most important functions or tasks that select deities had was to watch over and take care of music, sexual intercourse, and victory: human and devine actions and experiences which were to be boons to existence. Less important deities (and human beings) concerned themselves with basket-weaving, cloth making, and leather working: they were the laborers and not the nobility of either status.[25]

Once a god/goddess (or wo/man) was assigned
to his/her task they carried that appointment for
life.[26] They could not leave it and go to another,
for job mobility appeared as a form of instability
which was not tolerated in either world.[27]

Later, when New Babylon conquered Israel and
made Israel subject to her will, Israel recoiled
when many of her own people found comfort and
similarity with the Babylonian culture and
civilization, leading many xenophobes to lament
their existence in the Babylonian empire, and
later rejoice when it fell, as the psalmist sung:

By the river of Babylon, there we sat down,
yes, we wept, when we remembered Zion. .... If I
forget you, O Jerusalem, let my right hand forget
her cunning. ... O daughter of Babylon, who art
to be destroyed: happy shall he be, that rewards
you as you have served us.[28]

The urgency of the feeling was only
one-sided, for the Babylonians could not
understand why any person would want to be
anywhere other than Babylon. The Babylonian king
was powerful, prosperity abounded. And as the
Hebrews became more disquieted and turned to
clandestine activities including raids on
Babylonian military and citizens, the situation
became acute. The clearest record we have of it
is the text of the Book of Esther:

אֶסְתֵּר

When Ahasuerus reigned
from India to Ethiopia,
over one hundred and
twenty seven provinces, it
occurred in his palace
Shushan while he sat on
the throne in the third
year of his reign that he
prepared a party for all
of his princes and those
who served him in
the kingdom, including the
powers of Persia and
Media, and the nobles and
princes of the provinces.

They all came and
stood before him, and he
showed them the riches of
his glorious kingdom and
honor his majesty for many
days, even for one hundred
and eighty days. And, when
these days were over
the king offered a feast
for all the people that
were there in the Shushan
palace: both the great and
the small [for] seven
days. It was held in the
court garden of the king's
palace where there were
white, green, and blue
hangings which were
fastened with cords of
fine linen dyed purple
[which were fastened] to
silver rings and [then to]
marble pillars. The beds

וַיְהִי בִּימֵי אֲחַשְׁוֵרוֹשׁ הוּא אֲחַשְׁוֵרוֹשׁ
הַמֹּלֵךְ מֵהֹדּוּ וְעַד־כּוּשׁ שֶׁבַע
וְעֶשְׂרִים וּמֵאָה מְדִינָה: בַּיָּמִים הָהֵם
כְּשֶׁבֶת ׀ הַמֶּלֶךְ אֲחַשְׁוֵרוֹשׁ עַל כִּסֵּא
מַלְכוּתוֹ אֲשֶׁר בְּשׁוּשַׁן הַבִּירָה: בִּשְׁנַת
שָׁלוֹשׁ לְמָלְכוֹ עָשָׂה מִשְׁתֶּה לְכָל־שָׂרָיו
וַעֲבָדָיו חֵיל ׀ פָּרַס וּמָדַי הַפַּרְתְּמִים וְשָׂרֵי
הַמְּדִינוֹת לְפָנָיו: בְּהַרְאֹתוֹ אֶת־עֹשֶׁר
כְּבוֹד מַלְכוּתוֹ וְאֶת־יְקָר תִּפְאֶרֶת גְּדוּלָּתוֹ
יָמִים רַבִּים שְׁמוֹנִים וּמְאַת יוֹם: וּבִמְלוֹאת ׀
הַיָּמִים הָאֵלֶּה עָשָׂה הַמֶּלֶךְ לְכָל־הָעָם
הַנִּמְצְאִים בְּשׁוּשַׁן הַבִּירָה לְמִגָּדוֹל וְעַד־
קָטָן מִשְׁתֶּה שִׁבְעַת יָמִים בַּחֲצַר גִּנַּת
בִּיתַן הַמֶּלֶךְ: חוּר ׀ כַּרְפַּס וּתְכֵלֶת
אָחוּז בְּחַבְלֵי־בוּץ וְאַרְגָּמָן עַל־גְּלִילֵי כֶסֶף
וְעַמּוּדֵי שֵׁשׁ מִטּוֹת ׀ זָהָב וָכֶסֶף עַל
רִצְפַת בַּהַט־וָשֵׁשׁ וְדַר וְסֹחָרֶת: וְהַשְׁקוֹת

*ΚAI ἐγένετο μετὰ τοὺς λόγους τούτους ἐν
ταῖς ἡμέραις Ἀρταξέρξου, οὗτος ὁ Ἀρταξέρξης
ἀπὸ τῆς Ἰνδικῆς ἑκατὸν εἰκοσιεπτὰ χωρῶν ἐκρά-
τησεν. Ἐν αὐταῖς ταῖς ἡμέραις ὅτε ἐθρονίσθη
βασιλεὺς Ἀρταξέρξης ἐν Σούσοις τῇ πόλει, Ἐν
τῷ τρίτῳ ἔτει βασιλεύοντος αὐτοῦ, δοχὴν ἐποίησε
τοῖς φίλοις καὶ τοῖς λοιποῖς ἔθνεσι καὶ τοῖς
Περσῶν καὶ Μήδων ἐνδόξοις καὶ τοῖς ἄρχουσι τῶν
σατραπῶν. Καὶ μετὰ ταῦτα μετὰ τὸ δεῖξαι
αὐτοῖς τὸν πλοῦτον τῆς βασιλείας αὐτοῦ καὶ τὴν
δόξαν τῆς εὐφροσύνης τοῦ πλούτου αὐτοῦ ἐν
ἡμέραις ἑκατὸν ὀγδοήκοντα· Ὅτε δὲ ἀνεπληρώ-
θησαν αἱ ἡμέραι τοῦ γάμου, ἐποίησεν ὁ βασιλεὺς
πότον τοῖς ἔθνεσι τοῖς εὑρεθεῖσιν εἰς τὴν πόλιν
ἐπὶ ἡμέρας ἓξ ἐν αὐλῇ οἴκου τοῦ βασιλέως,
Κεκοσμημένῃ βυσσίνοις καὶ καρπασίνοις τεταμί-
νοις ἐπὶ σχοινίοις βυσσίνοις καὶ πορφυροῖς, ἐπὶ
κύβοις χρυσοῖς καὶ ἀργυροῖς, ἐπὶ στύλοις παρίνοις
καὶ λιθίνοις· κλῖναι χρυσαῖ καὶ ἀργυραῖ ἐπὶ
λιθοστρώτου σμαραγδίτου λίθου καὶ πιννίνου καὶ
παρίνου λίθου, καὶ στρωμναὶ διαφανεῖς ποικίλως
διηνθισμέναι, κύκλῳ ῥόδα πεπασμένα· Ποτήρια

Lon which the guests lounged] were [made] of gold and silver, and were on a pavement of red and blue and white and black marble. And they [the Babylonians] gave them [the guests] drink [poured out of jugs] in[to] chalices of gold, and they were very different from one another. There was an abundance of royal wine as would be the case with any asking. The drinking was according to the law, and no one was forced to indulge, for the king had ordered his servants to allow each guest to follow his own conscience. At the same time Queen Vashti made a [separate] feast for the women in king Ahasuerus' house.

Seven days later when the heart of the king was happy with the wine, he commanded Mehuman, Bizathe, Harbona, Bigtha, and Abagtha, Zethar, Carcas, the seven chamberlains that served [his guests], to bring Queen Vashti to him, now, wearing the royal crown-- to show the princes and the people her beauty, for she was attractive; but

בִּכְלֵי זָהָב וְכֵלִים מִכֵּלִים שׁוֹנִים וְיֵין מַלְכוּת רָב כְּיַד הַמֶּלֶךְ: וְהַשְּׁתִיָּה כַדָּת אֵין אֹנֵס כִּי־כֵן ׀ יִסַּד הַמֶּלֶךְ עַל כָּל־ רַב בֵּיתוֹ לַעֲשׂוֹת כִּרְצוֹן אִישׁ־וָאִישׁ: גַּם וַשְׁתִּי הַמַּלְכָּה עָשְׂתָה מִשְׁתֵּה נָשִׁים בֵּית הַמַּלְכוּת אֲשֶׁר לַמֶּלֶךְ אֲחַשְׁוֵרוֹשׁ: בַּיּוֹם הַשְּׁבִיעִי כְּטוֹב לֵב־ הַמֶּלֶךְ בַּיָּיִן אָמַר לִמְהוּמָן בִּזְּתָא חַרְבוֹנָא בִּגְתָא וַאֲבַגְתָא זֵתַר וְכַרְכַּס שִׁבְעַת הַסָּרִיסִים הַמְשָׁרְתִים אֶת־פְּנֵי הַמֶּלֶךְ אֲחַשְׁוֵרוֹשׁ: לְהָבִיא אֶת־וַשְׁתִּי הַמַּלְכָּה לִפְנֵי הַמֶּלֶךְ בְּכֶתֶר מַלְכוּת לְהַרְאוֹת הָעַמִּים וְהַשָּׂרִים אֶת־יָפְיָהּ כִּי־טוֹבַת מַרְאֶה הִיא: וַתְּמָאֵן הַמַּלְכָּה וַשְׁתִּי לָבוֹא בִּדְבַר הַמֶּלֶךְ אֲשֶׁר בְּיַד הַסָּרִיסִים וַיִּקְצֹף הַמֶּלֶךְ מְאֹד וַחֲמָתוֹ בָּעֲרָה בוֹ:

χρυσᾶ καὶ ἀργυρᾶ, καὶ ἀνθράκινον κυλίκιον προκείμενον ἀπὸ ταλάντων τρισμυρίων· οἶνος πολὺς
καὶ ἡδύς, ὃν αὐτὸς ὁ βασιλεὺς ἔπινεν. Ὁ δὲ
πότος οὗτος οὐ κατὰ προκείμενον νόμον ἐγένετο·
οὕτως δὲ ἠθέλησεν ὁ βασιλεύς, καὶ ἐπέταξε τοῖς
οἰκονόμοις ποιῆσαι τὸ θέλημα αὐτοῦ καὶ τῶν
ἀνθρώπων. Καὶ Ἀστὶν ἡ βασίλισσα ἐποίησε
πότον ταῖς γυναιξὶν ἐν τοῖς βασιλείοις ὅπου ὁ
βασιλεὺς Ἀρταξέρξης. Ἐν δὲ τῇ ἡμέρᾳ τῇ
ἑβδόμῃ ἡδέως γενόμενος ὁ βασιλεὺς εἶπε τῷ Ἀμὰν
καὶ Βαζὰν καὶ Θαρρὰ καὶ Βαραζὶ καὶ Ζαθολθᾶ
καὶ Ἀβαταζᾶ καὶ Θαραβᾶ, τοῖς ἑπτὰ εὐνούχοις
τοῖς διακόνοις τοῦ βασιλέως Ἀρταξέρξου,
Εἰσαγαγὼν τὴν βασίλισσαν πρὸς αὐτόν, βασι-
λεύειν αὐτὴν καὶ περιθεῖναι αὐτῇ τὸ διάδημα καὶ
δεῖξαι αὐτὴν τοῖς ἄρχουσι καὶ τοῖς ἔθεσι τὸ
κάλλος αὐτῆς, ὅτι καλὴ ἦν. Καὶ οὐκ εἰσή-

Queen Vashti refused to come at the king's command sent by his chamberlains. It upset the king and made him resentful. He said to his counselors who understood the situation for such was the king's tradition with all who knew his law and his will and were next to him, being Carhena, Shethar, Admatha, Tarshish, and Memucan, the seven princes of Persia, and of the Media, which saw the king's face; they were to be numbered among the first in the Kingdom, and said, "What shall we do to Queen Vashti according to law since she has not kept the law which is to obey the commands of the king Ahasuerus [as was delivered] by the chamberlains?"

Memucan answered the king and the princes who were near him: "The Queen Vashti has not only gone against the king, but has also embarrassed the assembled princes, and too, all of the people that are in the kingdom of Ahasuerus. For this deed Queen has set a bad example to all of the

וַיֹּאמֶר הַמֶּלֶךְ לַחֲכָמִים יֹדְעֵי
הָעִתִּים כִּי־כֵן דְּבַר הַמֶּלֶךְ לִפְנֵי כָּל־יֹדְעֵי
דָּת וָדִין: וְהַקָּרֹב אֵלָיו כַּרְשְׁנָא שֵׁתָר
אַדְמָתָא תַרְשִׁישׁ מֶרֶס מַרְסְנָא מְמוּכָן
שִׁבְעַת שָׂרֵי פָּרַס וּמָדַי רֹאֵי פְּנֵי הַמֶּלֶךְ
הַיֹּשְׁבִים רִאשֹׁנָה בַּמַּלְכוּת: כְּדָת מַה־
לַעֲשׂוֹת בַּמַּלְכָּה וַשְׁתִּי עַל אֲשֶׁר לֹא־
עָשְׂתָה אֶת־מַאֲמַר הַמֶּלֶךְ אֲחַשְׁוֵרוֹשׁ בְּיַד
הַסָּרִיסִים: וַיֹּאמֶר מְומֻכָן לִפְנֵי
הַמֶּלֶךְ וְהַשָּׂרִים לֹא עַל־הַמֶּלֶךְ לְבַדּוֹ
עָוְתָה וַשְׁתִּי הַמַּלְכָּה כִּי עַל־כָּל־הַשָּׂרִים
וְעַל־כָּל־הָעַמִּים אֲשֶׁר בְּכָל־מְדִינוֹת הַמֶּלֶךְ
אֲחַשְׁוֵרוֹשׁ: כִּי־יֵצֵא דְבַר־הַמַּלְכָּה עַל־
כָּל־הַנָּשִׁים לְהַבְזוֹת בַּעְלֵיהֶן בְּעֵינֵיהֶן
בְּאָמְרָם הַמֶּלֶךְ אֲחַשְׁוֵרוֹשׁ אָמַר לְהָבִיא
אֶת־וַשְׁתִּי הַמַּלְכָּה לְפָנָיו וְלֹא־בָאָה:

κουσεν αὐτοῦ Ἀστὶν ἡ βασίλισσα ἐλθεῖν μετὰ τῶν
εὐνούχων· καὶ ἐλυπήθη ὁ βασιλεὺς καὶ ὠργίσθη,

Καὶ εἶπε τοῖς φίλοις αὐτοῦ Κατὰ ταῦτα ἐλάλησεν Ἀστὶν, ποιήσατε οὖν περὶ τούτου νόμον καὶ
κρίσιν. Καὶ προσῆλθεν αὐτῷ Ἀρκεσαῖος καὶ
Σαρσαθαῖος καὶ Μαλισεὰρ οἱ ἄρχοντες Περσῶν καὶ
Μήδων οἱ ἐγγὺς τοῦ βασιλέως, οἱ πρῶτοι παρα-
καθήμενοι τῷ βασιλεῖ, Καὶ ἀπήγγειλαν αὐτῷ
κατὰ τοὺς νόμους ὡς δεῖ ποιῆσαι Ἀστὶν τῇ βασιλίσσῃ, ὅτι οὐκ ἐποίησε τὰ ὑπὸ τοῦ βασιλέως
προσταχθέντα διὰ τῶν εὐνούχων. 16 Καὶ εἶπεν ὁ
Μουχαῖος πρὸς τὸν βασιλέα καὶ τοὺς ἄρχοντας
Οὐ τὸν βασιλέα μόνον ἠδίκησεν Ἀστὶν ἡ
βασίλισσα, ἀλλὰ καὶ πάντας τοὺς ἄρχοντας
καὶ τοὺς ἡγουμένους τοῦ βασιλέως. Καὶ γὰρ
διηγήσατο αὐτοῖς τὰ ῥήματα τῆς βασιλίσσης, καὶ
ὡς ἀντεῖπε τῷ βασιλεῖ. Ὡς οὖν ἀντεῖπε τῷ
βασιλεῖ Ἀρταξέρξῃ, Οὕτω σήμερον αἱ τυραν-

women in the land: so that they too shall despise their husbands in their eyes."

[Hearing this] the king Ahasuerus commanded Queen Vashti to be brought to him. Still she did not come. (So, too, shall the women of Persia and Media say to this day to all of the king's princes, when they have learned of the Queen's defiance, which will lead to too much contempt and defiance and anger.) [Another counsellor suggested] "If it please the king, let there be a command which shall also be written into the laws of the Persians and also the Medes that can never be altered, that Queen Vashti is never again to appear before King Ahasuerus; and [furthermore] let the king give her royal estate to another that is better [and more obedient] than she [is].

And when the king's decree (which he shall make) is published throughout his kingdom, all the wives shall give to their husbands honor, both to those who are great or small."

וְהַיּוֹם הַזֶּה תֹּאמַרְנָה ׀ שָׂרוֹת פָּרַס־
וּמָדַי אֲשֶׁר שָׁמְעוּ אֶת־דְּבַר הַמַּלְכָּה לְכֹל
שָׂרֵי הַמֶּלֶךְ וּכְדַי בִּזָּיוֹן וָקָצֶף: אִם־עַל־
הַמֶּלֶךְ טוֹב יֵצֵא דְבַר־מַלְכוּת מִלְּפָנָיו
וְיִכָּתֵב בְּדָתֵי פָרַס־וּמָדַי וְלֹא יַעֲבוֹר אֲשֶׁר
לֹא־תָבוֹא וַשְׁתִּי לִפְנֵי הַמֶּלֶךְ אֲחַשְׁוֵרוֹשׁ
וּמַלְכוּתָהּ יִתֵּן הַמֶּלֶךְ לִרְעוּתָהּ הַטּוֹבָה
מִמֶּנָּה: וְנִשְׁמַע פִּתְגָם הַמֶּלֶךְ אֲשֶׁר־
יַעֲשֶׂה בְּכָל־מַלְכוּתוֹ כִּי רַבָּה הִיא וְכָל־
הַנָּשִׁים יִתְּנוּ יְקָר לְבַעֲלֵיהֶן לְמִגָּדוֹל וְעַד־
קָטָן: וַיִּיטַב הַדָּבָר בְּעֵינֵי הַמֶּלֶךְ

νίδες αἱ λοιπαὶ τῶν ἀρχόντων Περσῶν καὶ Μήδων
ἀκούσασαι τὰ τῷ βασιλεῖ λεχθέντα ὑπ' αὐτῆς
τολμήσουσιν ὁμοίως ἀτιμάσαι τοὺς ἄνδρας αὐτῶν.

Εἰ οὖν δοκεῖ τῷ βασιλεῖ, προσταξάτω βασι
λικὸν καὶ γραφήτω κατὰ τοὺς νόμους Μήδων καὶ
Περσῶν, καὶ μὴ ἄλλως χρησάσθω, μηδὲ εἰσελθέτω
ἔτι ἡ βασίλισσα πρὸς αὐτόν, καὶ τὴν βασιλείαν
αὐτῆς δότω ὁ βασιλεὺς γυναικὶ κρείττονι αὐτῆς.

Καὶ ἀκουσθήτω ὁ νόμος ὁ ὑπὸ τοῦ βασιλέως
ὃν ἐὰν ποιῇ ἐν τῇ βασιλείᾳ αὐτοῦ· καὶ οὕτω
πᾶσαι αἱ γυναῖκες περιθήσουσι τιμὴν τοῖς ἀνδράσιν
ἑαυτῶν, ἀπὸ πτωχοῦ ἕως πλουσίου.   Καὶ

And this suggestion pleased the king and the other princes, so that the king did as Memucan had suggested, sending out letters to all of the provinces, written in every language spoken by all of the people of the empire, so that every man should be able to rule over his own house.

After this occurred King Ahasuerus felt better, and he remembered Vashti and what she had done to upset him, and also what he had just decreed as law. [Seeing the king's discomfort] the king's servants said to him, "Let there be fair young girls sought out for you, and let the king appoint officers in every province of the kingdom to gather together all of the young girls and bring them to Shushan palace, to the House of Women, and [let them be placed in] the custody of Hege the king's chamberlain and keeper of the women; and let their things for purification [of menstrual orders] be given to them. Then let the maiden which pleases the king become Queen, instead of Vashti." And this suggestion pleased the king, and he followed

וְהַשָּׂרִים וַיַּעַשׂ הַמֶּלֶךְ כִּדְבַר מְמוּכָן :
וַיִּשְׁלַח סְפָרִים אֶל־כָּל־מְדִינוֹת הַמֶּלֶךְ
אֶל־מְדִינָה וּמְדִינָה כִּכְתָבָהּ וְאֶל־עַם וָעָם
כִּלְשׁוֹנוֹ לִהְיוֹת כָּל־אִישׁ שֹׂרֵר בְּבֵיתוֹ
וּמְדַבֵּר כִּלְשׁוֹן עַמּוֹ :

אַחַר הַדְּבָרִים הָאֵלֶּה כְּשֹׁךְ חֲמַת הַמֶּלֶךְ
אֲחַשְׁוֵרוֹשׁ זָכַר אֶת־וַשְׁתִּי וְאֵת אֲשֶׁר־עָשָׂתָה
וְאֵת אֲשֶׁר־נִגְזַר עָלֶיהָ : וַיֹּאמְרוּ נַעֲרֵי
הַמֶּלֶךְ מְשָׁרְתָיו יְבַקְשׁוּ לַמֶּלֶךְ נְעָרוֹת
בְּתוּלֹת טוֹבוֹת מַרְאֶה : וְיַפְקֵד הַמֶּלֶךְ
פְּקִידִים בְּכָל־מְדִינוֹת מַלְכוּתוֹ וְיִקְבְּצוּ אֶת־
כָּל־נַעֲרָה בְתוּלָה טוֹבַת מַרְאֶה אֶל־שׁוּשַׁן
הַבִּירָה אֶל־בֵּית הַנָּשִׁים אֶל־יַד הֵגֶא סְרִיס
הַמֶּלֶךְ שֹׁמֵר הַנָּשִׁים וְנָתוֹן תַּמְרֻקֵיהֶן :
וְהַנַּעֲרָה אֲשֶׁר תִּיטַב בְּעֵינֵי הַמֶּלֶךְ

ἤρεσεν ὁ λόγος τῷ βασιλεῖ καὶ τοῖς ἄρχουσι· καὶ
ἐποίησεν ὁ βασιλεὺς καθὰ ἐλάλησεν ὁ Μουχαῖος,

Καὶ ἀπέστειλεν εἰς πᾶσαν τὴν βασιλείαν κατὰ
χώραν, κατὰ τὴν λέξιν αὐτῶν, ὥστε εἶναι φόβον
αὐτοῖς ἐν ταῖς οἰκίαις αὐτῶν.

ΚΑΙ μετὰ τοὺς λόγους τουτους ἐκόπασεν ὁ
βασιλεὺς τοῦ θυμοῦ, καὶ οὐκ ἔτι ἐμνήσθη τῆς Αστίν,
μνημονεύων οἷα ἐλάλησε καὶ ὡς κατέκρινεν αὐτήν.

Καὶ εἶπαν οἱ διάκονοι τοῦ βασιλέως· Ζητηθήτω
τῷ βασιλεῖ κοράσια ἄφθορα καλὰ τῷ εἴδει· Καὶ
καταστήσει ὁ βασιλεὺς κωμάρχας ἐν πάσαις ταῖς
χώραις τῆς βασιλείας αὐτοῦ, καὶ ἐπιλεξάτωσαν
κοράσια παρθενικὰ καλὰ τῷ εἴδει εἰς Σοῦσαν τὴν
πόλιν εἰς τὸν γυναικῶνα, καὶ παραδοθήτωσαν τῷ
εὐνούχῳ τοῦ βασιλέως τῷ φύλακι τῶν γυναικῶν,
καὶ δοθήτω σμῆγμα καὶ ἡ λοιπὴ ἐπιμέλεια·

Καὶ ἡ γυνὴ ἣ ἂν ἀρέσῃ τῷ βασιλεῖ βασιλεύσει
ἀντὶ Αστίν. Καὶ ἤρεσε τῷ βασιλεῖ τὸ πρᾶγμα,

their advise.

Now in Shushan palace there was a certain Hebrew whose name was Mordecai, the son of Jair, the son of Shemei, the son of Kish, a Benjamite who had been carried away from Jerusalem with the captivity when Jeconiah, King of Judah, was carried off by the King of Babylon: Nebuchadnezzar. He [Mordecai] brought up Hadassah, or Esther, his uncle's daughter since she had neither a father or a mother. She was a fair and beautiful young girl, whom Mordecai took for his own daughter when her parents died.

תִּמָּלֵךְ תַּחַת וַשְׁתִּי וַיִּיטַב הַדָּבָר בְּעֵינֵי
הַמֶּלֶךְ וַיַּעַשׂ כֵּן : אִישׁ יְהוּדִי
הָיָה בְּשׁוּשַׁן הַבִּירָה וּשְׁמוֹ מָרְדֳּכַי בֶּן
יָאִיר בֶּן־שִׁמְעִי בֶּן־קִישׁ אִישׁ יְמִינִי :
אֲשֶׁר הָגְלָה מִירוּשָׁלַיִם עִם־הַגֹּלָה אֲשֶׁר
הָגְלְתָה עִם יְכָנְיָה מֶלֶךְ־יְהוּדָה אֲשֶׁר
הֶגְלָה נְבוּכַדְנֶצַּר מֶלֶךְ בָּבֶל : וַיְהִי אֹמֵן
אֶת־הֲדַסָּה הִיא אֶסְתֵּר בַּת־דֹּדוֹ כִּי אֵין
לָהּ אָב וָאֵם וְהַנַּעֲרָה יְפַת־תֹּאַר וְטוֹבַת
מַרְאֶה וּבְמוֹת אָבִיהָ וְאִמָּהּ לְקָחָהּ מָרְדֳּכַי
לוֹ לְבַת : וַיְהִי בְּהִשָּׁמַע דְּבַר־הַמֶּלֶךְ

**Sargon I of Akkad
(Reigned c. 2800 B. C.)**
The superbly cast bronze head, found at Nineveh, was probably damaged by thieves gouging out gems inset in the eye sockets.
Hirmer Fotoarchiv

καὶ ἐποίησεν οὕτως. Καὶ ἄνθρωπος ἦν Ἰου
δαῖος ἐν Σούσοις τῇ πόλει, καὶ ὄνομα αὐτοῦ
Μαρδοχαῖος ὁ τοῦ Ἰαΐρου τοῦ Σεμεΐου τοῦ Κισαίου,
ἐκ φυλῆς Βενιαμίν, Ὃς ἦν αἰχμάλωτος ἐξ
Ἰερουσαλὴμ ἦν ᾐχμαλώτευσε Ναβουχοδονόσορ
βασιλεὺς Βαβυλῶνος. Καὶ ἦν τούτῳ παῖς
θρεπτή, θυγάτηρ Ἀμιναδὰβ ἀδελφοῦ πατρὸς αὐτοῦ,
καὶ ὄνομα αὐτῇ Ἐσθήρ· ἐν δὲ τῷ μεταλλάξαι
αὐτῆς τοὺς γονεῖς ἐπαίδευσεν αὐτὴν ἑαυτῷ εἰς
γυναῖκα· καὶ ἦν τὸ κοράσιον καλὸν τῷ εἴδει.

So it happened that when the king's command was heard many young girls assembled and went to Shushan Palace, entering into the custody of Hege, the keeper of the the women. And Esther was in that number.

Esther pleased Hege, and he rewarded her by doing kind things for her, including getting for Esther items for her purification; and he did it quickly, bringing to her the things which were already hers. Then [he selected] seven young girls to attend her, bringing them from the king's house, and gave to Esther and to her attendants the best place in the House of Women.

During this time the young girl Esther did not tell anyone that she was a Hebrew. Mordecai had warned her against it. [Worried about her safety and comfort] Mordecai walked every day in front of the court of the House of Women to learn how Esther was doing, and what was to become of her. When it was the time for every maid to come before the king Ahasuerus (after she had been

וַיְהִי בְּהִקָּבֵץ נְעָרוֹת רַבּוֹת אֶל־שׁוּשָׁן
הַבִּירָה אֶל־יַד הֵגַי וַתִּלָּקַח אֶסְתֵּר אֶל־
בֵּית הַמֶּלֶךְ אֶל־יַד הֵגַי שֹׁמֵר הַנָּשִׁים:
וַתִּיטַב הַנַּעֲרָה בְעֵינָיו וַתִּשָּׂא חֶסֶד
לְפָנָיו וַיְבַהֵל אֶת־תַּמְרוּקֶיהָ וְאֶת־
מָנוֹתֶהָ לָתֵת לָהּ וְאֵת שֶׁבַע הַנְּעָרוֹת
הָרְאֻיוֹת לָתֶת־לָהּ מִבֵּית הַמֶּלֶךְ וַיְשַׁנֶּהָ
וְאֶת־נַעֲרוֹתֶיהָ ∙ לְטוֹב בֵּית הַנָּשִׁים:
לֹא־הִגִּידָה אֶסְתֵּר אֶת־עַמָּהּ וְאֶת־מוֹלַדְתָּהּ
כִּי מָרְדֳּכַי צִוָּה עָלֶיהָ אֲשֶׁר לֹא־תַגִּיד:
וּבְכָל־יוֹם וָיוֹם מָרְדֳּכַי מִתְהַלֵּךְ לִפְנֵי
חֲצַר בֵּית־הַנָּשִׁים לָדַעַת אֶת־שְׁלוֹם אֶסְתֵּר
וּמַה־יֵּעָשֶׂה בָּהּ: וּבְהַגִּיעַ תֹּר נַעֲרָה
וְנַעֲרָה לָבוֹא ∙ אֶל־הַמֶּלֶךְ אֲחַשְׁוֵרוֹשׁ מִקֵּץ
הֱיוֹת לָהּ כְּדָת הַנָּשִׁים שְׁנֵים עָשָׂר חֹדֶשׁ
כִּי כֵּן יִמְלְאוּ יְמֵי מְרוּקֵיהֶן שִׁשָּׁה חֳדָשִׁים
בְּשֶׁמֶן הַמֹּר וְשִׁשָּׁה חֳדָשִׁים בַּבְּשָׂמִים

Καὶ ὅτε ἠκούσθη τὸ τοῦ βασιλέως πρόσταγμα,
συνήχθησαν πολλὰ κοράσια εἰς Σοῦσαν τὴν πόλιν
ὑπὸ χεῖρα Γαί, καὶ ἤχθη Ἐσθὴρ πρὸς Γαί τὸν
φύλακα τῶν γυναικῶν.   Καὶ ἤρεσεν αὐτῷ τὸ
κοράσιον, καὶ εὗρε χάριν ἐνώπιον αὐτοῦ· καὶ
ἔσπευσε δοῦναι αὐτῇ τὸ σμῆγμα καὶ τὴν μερίδα
καὶ τὰ ἑπτὰ κοράσια τὰ ὑποδεδειγμένα αὐτῇ ἐκ
βασιλικοῦ, καὶ ἐχρήσατο αὐτῇ καλῶς καὶ ταῖς
ἅβραις αὐτῆς ἐν τῷ γυναικῶνι.   Καὶ οὐχ
ὑπέδειξεν Ἐσθὴρ τὸ γένος αὐτῆς οὐδὲ τὴν πατρίδα·
ὁ γὰρ Μαρδοχαῖος ἐνετείλατο αὐτῇ μὴ ἀπαγγεῖλαι.
    Καθ᾽ ἑκάστην δὲ ἡμέραν περιεπάτει ὁ Μαρ-
δοχαῖος κατὰ τὴν αὐλὴν τὴν γυναικείαν, ἐπι-
σκοπῶν τί Ἐσθὴρ συμβήσεται.   Οὗτος δὲ ἦν
καιρὸς κορασίου εἰσελθεῖν πρὸς τὸν βασιλέα, ὅταν
ἀναπληρώσῃ μῆνας δεκαδύο· οὕτως γὰρ ἀναπλη-
ροῦνται αἱ ἡμέραι τῆς θεραπείας, μῆνας ϛ̄
ἀλειφομέναις ἐν σμυρνίνῳ ἐλαίῳ, καὶ μῆνας ϛ̄ ἐν
τοῖς ἀρώμασι καὶ ἐν τοῖς σμήγμασι τῶν γυναικῶν,

confined for twelve
months, according to the
custom of women at that
time, for so were the days
of their purification ac-
complished, to wit, six
months with oil of myrrh,
and six months with sweet
odors, and with other
things used for the purify-
ing of women), each maid
appeared in turn, and she
was given whatever she desired out of the House of
Women to take to the
king's house.

Each girl went in
the evening, and in the
morning returned to the
House of Women, to the custody of Shaashgaz, the
king's chamberlain which
kept the concubines [who
had slept with the king]
and she saw the king no
more unless the king called her by name because she
had pleased him [during
the night].

When Esther's turn
came (she was the daughter
of Abihail, the uncle of
Mordecai who had taken her
for his daughter) to go to
the king, she [declared]
that she needed nothing
but what Hege, the king's
chamberlain and keeper of
the women, decided she
should take.

וּבְהַמְרֻקֵי הַנָּשִׁים : וּבָזֶה הַנַּעֲרָה בָּאָה
אֶל־הַמֶּלֶךְ אֵת כָּל־אֲשֶׁר תֹּאמַר יִנָּתֵן לָהּ
לָבוֹא עִמָּהּ מִבֵּית הַנָּשִׁים עַד־בֵּית
הַמֶּלֶךְ : בָּעֶרֶב ׀ הִיא בָאָה וּבַבֹּקֶר הִיא
שָׁבָה אֶל־בֵּית הַנָּשִׁים שֵׁנִי אֶל־יַד שַׁעֲשְׁגַז
סְרִיס הַמֶּלֶךְ שֹׁמֵר הַפִּילַגְשִׁים לֹא־תָבוֹא
עוֹד אֶל־הַמֶּלֶךְ כִּי אִם־חָפֵץ בָּהּ הַמֶּלֶךְ
וְנִקְרְאָה בְשֵׁם : וּבְהַגִּיעַ תֹּר־אֶסְתֵּר בַּת־
אֲבִיחַיִל ׀ דֹּד מָרְדֳּכַי אֲשֶׁר לָקַח־לוֹ לְבַת
לָבוֹא אֶל־הַמֶּלֶךְ לֹא בִקְשָׁה דָּבָר כִּי אִם
אֶת־אֲשֶׁר יֹאמַר הֵגַי סְרִיס־הַמֶּלֶךְ שֹׁמֵר
הַנָּשִׁים וַתְּהִי אֶסְתֵּר נֹשֵׂאת חֵן בְּעֵינֵי

Καὶ τότε εἰσπορεύεται πρὸς τὸν βασιλέα· καὶ
ᾧ ἐὰν εἴπῃ, παραδώσει αὐτὴν συνεισέρχεσθαι αὐτῷ
ἀπὸ τοῦ γυναικῶνος ἕως τῶν βασιλείων. Δείλης
εἰσπορεύεται, καὶ πρὸς ἡμέραν ἀποτρέχει εἰς τὸν
γυναικῶνα τὸν δεύτερον οὗ Γαῖ ὁ εὐνοῦχος τοῦ
βασιλέως ὁ φύλαξ τῶν γυναικῶν, καὶ οὐκ ἔτι
εἰσπορεύεται πρὸς τὸν βασιλέα ἐὰν μὴ κληθῇ
ὀνόματι. Ἐν δὲ τῷ ἀναπληροῦσθαι τὸν χρόν:ν
Ἐσθὴρ τῆς θυγατρὸς Ἀμιναδὰβ ἀδελφοῦ πατρὸς
Μαρδοχαίου εἰσελθεῖν πρὸς τὸν βασιλέα, οὐδὲν ἠθέτη-
σεν ὧν ἐνετείλατο ὁ εὐνοῦχος ὁ φύλαξ τῶν γυναικῶν·
ἦν γὰρ Ἐσθὴρ εὑρίσκουσα χάριν παρὰ πάντων τῶν
βλεπόντων αὐτήν. Καὶ εἰσῆλθεν Ἐσθὴρ πρὸς

38

For this reason Esther obtained popularity in the estimation of all who knew her and looked upon her. So Esther was taken into the royal house of King Ahasuerus in the tenth month (which is the month of Tebeth) in the seventh year of his reign).

The king loved the girl Esther above all of the women, and she did obtain grace and favor in his sight above all of the other young girls, so much so that he set the royal crown upon her head and made her queen instead of Vashti. To celebrate this the king a great dinner party, and invited all of his princes and advisers, and [going against custom] he even invited Esther. He also gave special benefits to the provinces, and even gave out gifts which were in keeping with his status of being a king. (And when the young girls gathered to celebrate, Mordecai sat in the [*janu*] king's main gateway.) Still Esther did not tell anyone of the origin of her heritage, as Mordecai had charged her when she

כָּל־רֹאֶיהָ : וַתִּלָּקַח אֶסְתֵּר אֶל־הַמֶּלֶךְ
אֲחַשְׁוֵרוֹשׁ אֶל־בֵּית מַלְכוּתוֹ בַּחֹדֶשׁ הָעֲשִׂירִי
הוּא־חֹדֶשׁ טֵבֵת בִּשְׁנַת־שֶׁבַע לְמַלְכוּתוֹ :
וַיֶּאֱהַב הַמֶּלֶךְ אֶת־אֶסְתֵּר מִכָּל־הַנָּשִׁים
וַתִּשָּׂא־חֵן וָחֶסֶד לְפָנָיו מִכָּל־הַבְּתוּלוֹת
וַיָּשֶׂם כֶּתֶר־מַלְכוּת בְּרֹאשָׁהּ וַיַּמְלִיכֶהָ תַּחַת
וַשְׁתִּי : וַיַּעַשׂ הַמֶּלֶךְ מִשְׁתֶּה גָדוֹל
לְכָל־שָׂרָיו וַעֲבָדָיו אֵת מִשְׁתֵּה אֶסְתֵּר
וַהֲנָחָה לַמְּדִינוֹת עָשָׂה וַיִּתֵּן מַשְׂאֵת כְּיַד
הַמֶּלֶךְ : וּבְהִקָּבֵץ בְּתוּלוֹת שֵׁנִית
וּמָרְדֳּכַי יֹשֵׁב בְּשַׁעַר־הַמֶּלֶךְ : אֵין אֶסְתֵּר
מַגֶּדֶת מוֹלַדְתָּהּ וְאֶת־עַמָּהּ כַּאֲשֶׁר צִוָּה
עָלֶיהָ מָרְדֳּכָי וְאֶת־מַאֲמַר מָרְדֳּכַי אֶסְתֵּר
עֹשָׂה כַּאֲשֶׁר הָיְתָה בְאָמְנָה אִתּוֹ :
בַּיָּמִים הָהֵם וּמָרְדֳּכַי יֹשֵׁב בְּשַׁעַר־הַמֶּלֶךְ
קָצַף בִּגְתָן וָתֶרֶשׁ שְׁנֵי־סָרִיסֵי הַמֶּלֶךְ
מִשֹּׁמְרֵי הַסַּף וַיְבַקְשׁוּ לִשְׁלֹחַ יָד בַּמֶּלֶךְ

Ἀρταξέρξην τὸν βασιλέα τῷ δωδεκάτῳ μηνὶ ὅς ἐστιν Ἀδάρ, τῷ ἑβδόμῳ ἔτει τῆς βασιλείας αὐτοῦ.

Καὶ ἠράσθη ὁ βασιλεὺς Ἐσθήρ, καὶ εὗρε χάριν παρὰ πάσας τὰς παρθένους, καὶ ἐπέθηκεν αὐτῇ τὸ διάδημα τὸ γυναικεῖον. Καὶ ἐποίησεν ὁ βασιλεὺς πότον πᾶσι τοῖς φίλοις αὐτοῦ καὶ ταῖς δυνάμεσιν ἐπὶ ἡμέρας ἑπτά, καὶ ὕψωσε τοὺς γάμους Ἐσθήρ, καὶ ἄφεσιν ἐποίησε τοῖς ὑπὸ τὴν βασιλείαν αὐτοῦ. Ὁ δὲ Μαρδοχαῖος ἐθεράπευεν ἐν τῇ αὐλῇ. Ἡ δὲ Ἐσθὴρ οὐχ ὑπέδειξε τὴν πατρίδα αὐτῆς· οὕτως γὰρ ἐνετείλατο αὐτῇ Μαρδοχαῖος, φοβεῖσθαι τὸν θεὸν καὶ ποιεῖν τὰ προστάγματα αὐτοῦ, καθὼς ἦν μετ' αὐτοῦ· καὶ Ἐσθὴρ οὐ μετήλλαξε τὴν ἀγωγὴν αὐτῆς. Καὶ ἐλυπή-θησαν οἱ δύο εὐνοῦχοι τοῦ βασιλέως οἱ ἀρχισω-ματοφύλακες ὅτι προήχθη Μαρδοχαῖος, καὶ ἐζήτουν ἀποκτεῖναι Ἀρταξέρξην τὸν βασιλέα. Καὶ

had lived with him.

At the same time, while Mordecai sat in the king's gateway, two of the king's chamberlains by the names of Bigthan and Teresh, who stood on guard at the [capital?] gate where the king's advisers stood where Mordecai sat, [discussing how they] sought to overthrow King Ahasuerus and this became known to Mordecai who relayed the information to Queen Esther; and Esther certified the king of this information giving credit Mordecai. An investigation was made of this charge, and when it was learned to be true the two conspirators were both hanged from a tree (as recorded in the Book of Chronicles). And the king watched.

After this happened the King Ahasuerus promoted Haman, the son of Hammedatha the Agagite, and advanced him to the Position where he sat at the head of all of the other princes. When this happened all of the servants of the king who were at the gate bowed and showed him reverence, all except Mordecai who would

אֲחַשְׁוֵרֹשׁ : וַיִּוָּדַע הַדָּבָר לְמָרְדֳּכַי וַיַּגֵּד לְאֶסְתֵּר הַמַּלְכָּה וַתֹּאמֶר אֶסְתֵּר לַמֶּלֶךְ בְּשֵׁם מָרְדֳּכָי : וַיְבֻקַּשׁ הַדָּבָר וַיִּמָּצֵא וַיִּתָּלוּ שְׁנֵיהֶם עַל־עֵץ וַיִּכָּתֵב בְּסֵפֶר דִּבְרֵי הַיָּמִים לִפְנֵי הַמֶּלֶךְ :

אַחַר ׀ הַדְּבָרִים הָאֵלֶּה גִּדַּל הַמֶּלֶךְ אֲחַשְׁוֵרֹשׁ אֶת־הָמָן בֶּן־הַמְּדָתָא הָאֲגָגִי וַיְנַשְּׂאֵהוּ וַיָּשֶׂם אֶת־כִּסְאוֹ מֵעַל כָּל־ הַשָּׂרִים אֲשֶׁר אִתּוֹ : וְכָל־עַבְדֵי הַמֶּלֶךְ

ἐδηλώθη Μαρδοχαίῳ ὁ λόγος, καὶ ἐσήμανεν Ἐσθήρ, καὶ αὐτὴ ἐνεφάνησε τῷ βασιλεῖ τὰ τῆς ἐπιβουλῆς.

Ὁ δὲ βασιλεὺς ἤτασε τοὺς δύο εὐνούχους καὶ ἐκρέμασεν αὐτούς· καὶ προσέταξεν ὁ βασιλεὺς καταχωρίσαι εἰς μνημόσυνον ἐν τῇ βασιλικῇ βιβλιοθήκῃ ὑπὲρ τῆς εὐνοίας Μαρδοχαίου ἐν ἐγκωμίῳ.

ΜΕΤΑ δὲ ταῦτα ἐδόξασεν ὁ βασιλεὺς Ἀρταξέρξης Ἀμὰν Ἀμαδάθου Βουγαῖον, καὶ ὕψωσεν αὐτὸν καὶ ἐπρωτοβάθρει πάντων τῶν φίλων αὐτοῦ·

not bow but did acknowledge his elevation with reverence. The servants of the king who were at the gate questioned Mordecai, "Why are you disobeying the king's order?" [Mordecai did not respond], and they continued to question him in the same manner daily, [*each day*] but he would not listen to them, so they told Haman that Mordecai was a Hebrew, as he had told them, and they wanted to see where [Haman] stood [on tolerating Hebrews].

When Haman saw that Mordecai did not bow before him, nor reverenced him, Haman became angry, yet he was hesitant to harm him alone since the servants told him he was a Hebrew [and there were many Hebrews in Babylon, so many that Haman] had the desire to destroy all Hebrews that were in the kingdom of [*the King*] Ahasuerus, including the family of Mordecai. In the first month, the month of Nisan, in the twelfth year of King Ahasuerus, they cast Pur, that is, the lot [the temptation], before Haman, from day to day and month to month, to the twelfth month, that is

אֲשֶׁר־בְּשַׁעַר הַמֶּלֶךְ כֹּרְעִים וּמִשְׁתַּחֲוִים
לְהָמָן כִּי־כֵן צִוָּה־לוֹ הַמֶּלֶךְ וּמָרְדֳּכַי לֹא
יִכְרַע וְלֹא יִשְׁתַּחֲוֶה: וַיֹּאמְרוּ עַבְדֵי
הַמֶּלֶךְ אֲשֶׁר־בְּשַׁעַר הַמֶּלֶךְ לְמָרְדֳּכָי מַדּוּעַ
אַתָּה עוֹבֵר אֵת מִצְוַת הַמֶּלֶךְ: וַיְהִי
בְּאָמְרָם אֵלָיו יוֹם וָיוֹם וְלֹא שָׁמַע אֲלֵיהֶם
וַיַּגִּידוּ לְהָמָן לִרְאוֹת הֲיַעַמְדוּ דִּבְרֵי מָרְדֳּכַי
כִּי־הִגִּיד לָהֶם אֲשֶׁר־הוּא יְהוּדִי: וַיַּרְא
הָמָן כִּי־אֵין מָרְדֳּכַי כֹּרֵעַ וּמִשְׁתַּחֲוֶה לוֹ
וַיִּמָּלֵא הָמָן חֵמָה: וַיִּבֶז בְּעֵינָיו לִשְׁלֹחַ יָד
בְּמָרְדֳּכַי לְבַדּוֹ כִּי־הִגִּידוּ לוֹ אֶת־עַם מָרְדֳּכָי
וַיְבַקֵּשׁ הָמָן לְהַשְׁמִיד אֶת־כָּל־הַיְּהוּדִים
אֲשֶׁר בְּכָל־מַלְכוּת אֲחַשְׁוֵרוֹשׁ עַם מָרְדֳּכָי:
בַּחֹדֶשׁ הָרִאשׁוֹן הוּא־חֹדֶשׁ נִיסָן בִּשְׁנַת
שְׁתֵּים עֶשְׂרֵה לַמֶּלֶךְ אֲחַשְׁוֵרוֹשׁ הִפִּיל פּוּר
הוּא הַגּוֹרָל לִפְנֵי הָמָן מִיּוֹם לְיוֹם וּמֵחֹדֶשׁ
לְחֹדֶשׁ שְׁנֵים־עָשָׂר הוּא־חֹדֶשׁ אֲדָר:

Καὶ πάντες οἱ ἐν τῇ αὐλῇ προσεκύνουν αὐτῷ,
οὕτως γὰρ προσέταξεν ὁ βασιλεὺς ποιῆσαι· ὁ δὲ
Μαρδοχαῖος οὐ προσεκύνει αὐτῷ. Καὶ ἐλάλησαν
οἱ ἐν τῇ αὐλῇ τοῦ βασιλέως τῷ Μαρδοχαίῳ
Μαρδοχαῖε, τί παρακούεις τὰ ὑπὸ τοῦ βασιλέως
λεγόμενα; Καθ' ἑκάστην ἡμέραν ἐλάλουν αὐτῷ,
καὶ οὐχ ὑπήκουεν αὐτῶν· καὶ ὑπέδειξαν τῷ Ἀμὰν
Μαρδοχαῖον τοῖς τοῦ βασιλέως λόγοις ἀντιτασ-
σόμενον, καὶ ὑπέδειξεν αὐτοῖς ὁ Μαρδοχαῖος ὅτι
Ἰουδαῖός ἐστι. Καὶ ἐπιγνοὺς Ἀμὰν ὅτι οὐ
προσκυνεῖ αὐτῷ Μαρδοχαῖος, ἐθυμώθη σφόδρα,
Καὶ ἐβουλεύσατο ἀφανίσαι πάντας τοὺς ὑπὸ
τὴν Ἀρταξέρξου βασιλείαν Ἰουδαίους. Καὶ
ἐποίησε ψήφισμα ἐν ἔτει δωδεκάτῳ τῆς βασιλείας
Ἀρταξέρξου, καὶ ἔβαλε κλήρους ἡμέραν ἐξ
ἡμέρας καὶ μῆνα ἐκ μηνὸς ὥστε ἀπολέσαι ἐν μιᾷ
ἡμέρᾳ τὸ γένος Μαρδοχαῖον, καὶ ἔπεσεν ὁ κλῆρος
εἰς τὴν τεσσαρεσκαιδεκάτην τοῦ μηνὸς ὅς ἐστιν Ἀδάρ.

to the month Adar. And Haman said unto the king Ahasuerus, "There is a certain people in all of the provinces of your kingdom whose laws are different than those of other citizens; and since they do not keep your laws it is of no profit to you. If you think that it is good I suggest that you order them to be destroyed, and I will pay ten thousand talents [i.e. unit of weight, usually a coin] of silver to those who execute the order, and bring it into the treasury of the king.

The king took his ring off of his finger and gave it to Haman, the son of Hammedatha the Agagite, who was the Jews enemy. Then Then the king said to Haman, "The silver is given to you, and so to you may do with the [Hebrew] people as you desire.

The king's secretaries were then called on the thirteenth day of the first month, and it was written as Haman wished, and as he had commanded the king's lieutenants, and to the governors that

וַיֹּאמֶר הָמָן לַמֶּלֶךְ אֲחַשְׁוֵרוֹשׁ
יֶשְׁנוֹ עַם־אֶחָד מְפֻזָּר וּמְפֹרָד בֵּין הָעַמִּים
בְּכֹל מְדִינוֹת מַלְכוּתֶךָ וְדָתֵיהֶם שֹׁנוֹת
מִכָּל־עָם וְאֶת־דָּתֵי הַמֶּלֶךְ אֵינָם עֹשִׂים
וְלַמֶּלֶךְ אֵין־שֹׁוֶה לְהַנִּיחָם: אִם־עַל־הַמֶּלֶךְ
טוֹב יִכָּתֵב לְאַבְּדָם וַעֲשֶׂרֶת אֲלָפִים כִּכַּר־
כֶּסֶף אֶשְׁקוֹל עַל־יְדֵי עֹשֵׂי הַמְּלָאכָה לְהָבִיא
אֶל־גִּנְזֵי הַמֶּלֶךְ: וַיָּסַר הַמֶּלֶךְ אֶת־
טַבַּעְתּוֹ מֵעַל יָדוֹ וַיִּתְּנָהּ לְהָמָן בֶּן־
הַמְּדָתָא הָאֲגָגִי צֹרֵר הַיְּהוּדִים: וַיֹּאמֶר
הַמֶּלֶךְ לְהָמָן הַכֶּסֶף נָתוּן לָךְ וְהָעָם
לַעֲשׂוֹת בּוֹ כַּטּוֹב בְּעֵינֶיךָ: וַיִּקָּרְאוּ
סֹפְרֵי הַמֶּלֶךְ בַּחֹדֶשׁ הָרִאשׁוֹן בִּשְׁלוֹשָׁה
עָשָׂר יוֹם בּוֹ וַיִּכָּתֵב כְּכָל־אֲשֶׁר־צִוָּה הָמָן
אֶל אֲחַשְׁדַּרְפְּנֵי־הַמֶּלֶךְ וְאֶל־הַפַּחוֹת אֲשֶׁר |
עַל־מְדִינָה וּמְדִינָה וְאֶל־שָׂרֵי עַם וָעָם
מְדִינָה וּמְדִינָה כִּכְתָבָהּ וְעַם וָעָם כִּלְשׁוֹנוֹ
בְּשֵׁם הַמֶּלֶךְ אֲחַשְׁוֵרֹשׁ נִכְתָּב וְנֶחְתָּם

Καὶ ἐλάλησε πρὸς τὸν βασιλέα Ἀρταξέρξην λέγων Ὑπάρχει ἔθνος διεσπαρμένον ἐν τοῖς ἔθνεσιν ἐν πάσῃ τῇ βασιλείᾳ σου, οἱ δὲ νόμοι αὐτῶν ἔξαλλοι παρὰ πάντα τὰ ἔθνη, τῶν δὲ νόμων τοῦ βασιλέως παρακούουσι, καὶ οὐ συμφέρει τῷ βασιλεῖ ἐᾶσαι αὐτούς. Εἰ δοκεῖ τῷ βασιλεῖ, δογμα-τισάτω ἀπολέσαι αὐτούς, κἀγὼ διαγράψω εἰς τὸ γαζοφυλάκιον τοῦ βασιλέως ἀργυρίου τάλαντα μύρια. Καὶ περιελόμενος ὁ βασιλεὺς τὸν δα-κτύλιον ἔδωκεν εἰς χεῖρας τῷ Ἀμάν, σφραγίσαι κατὰ τῶν γεγραμμένων κατὰ τῶν Ἰουδαίων.
Καὶ εἶπεν ὁ βασιλεὺς τῷ Ἀμάν Τὸ μὲν ἀργύριον ἔχε, τῷ δὲ ἔθνει χρῶ ὡς βούλει. Καὶ ἐκλήθησαν οἱ γραμματεῖς τοῦ βασιλέως μηνὶ πρώτῳ τῇ τρισκαιδεκάτῃ, καὶ ἔγραψαν ὡς ἐπέταξεν Ἀμὰν τοῖς στρατηγοῖς καὶ τοῖς ἄρχουσι κατὰ πᾶσαν χώραν ἀπὸ Ἰνδικῆς ἕως τῆς Αἰθιοπίας, ταῖς ἑκατὸν εἰκοσιεπτὰ χώραις, τοῖς τε ἄρχουσι τῶν ἐθνῶν κατὰ τὴν αὐτῶν λέξιν, διὰ Ἀρταξέρξου τοῦ

were over every province, and to the rulers of each people of every province, according to the new law; and, it was signed with the king's name, and it was sealed with the king's own ring. Then the letters were sent by messenger, being hastened by the king's own command, and the decree was given throughout Shushan Palace apartments. Then the king and Haman sat down to drink, while the palace worried.

When Mordecai understood what had happened he tore his clothes and put on sackcloth with ashes, and he went into the heart of the city and cried with a loud and a bitter cry, coming before the king's gate. Yet none may enter into the king's home wearing sackcloth. (And in every province where the king's decree was read there was a loud mourning among the Jews. They fasted, weeped, and wailed; many lay in sack cloth and ashes.)

Esther's maids and servants came and told her about Mordecai, and the queen was greived greatly. She sent new

בְּטַבַּעַת הַמֶּֽלֶךְ׃ וְנִשְׁלֹ֣וֹחַ סְפָרִים֮ בְּיַ֣ד הָרָצִים֒ אֶל־כָּל־מְדִינ֣וֹת הַמֶּ֔לֶךְ לְהַשְׁמִ֡יד לַהֲרֹ֣ג וּלְאַבֵּ֡ד אֶת־כָּל־הַ֠יְּהוּדִים מִנַּ֨עַר וְעַד־ זָקֵ֜ן טַ֤ף וְנָשִׁים֙ בְּי֣וֹם אֶחָ֔ד בִּשְׁלוֹשָׁ֥ה עָשָׂ֛ר לְחֹ֥דֶשׁ שְׁנֵים־עָשָׂ֖ר הוּא־חֹ֣דֶשׁ אֲדָ֑ר וּשְׁלָלָ֖ם לָבֽוֹז׃ פַּתְשֶׁ֣גֶן הַכְּתָ֗ב לְהִנָּ֤תֵֽן דָּת֙ בְּכָל־ מְדִינָ֣ה וּמְדִינָ֔ה גָּל֖וּי לְכָל־הָעַמִּ֑ים לִהְי֥וֹת עֲתִדִ֖ים לַיּ֥וֹם הַזֶּֽה׃ הָרָצִ֞ים יָצְא֤וּ דְחוּפִים֙ בִּדְבַ֣ר הַמֶּ֔לֶךְ וְהַדָּ֥ת נִתְּנָ֖ה בְּשׁוּשַׁ֣ן הַבִּירָ֑ה וְהַמֶּ֤לֶךְ וְהָמָן֙ יָשְׁב֣וּ לִשְׁתּ֔וֹת וְהָעִ֥יר שׁוּשָׁ֖ן נָבֽוֹכָה׃

וּמָרְדֳּכַ֗י יָדַע֙ אֶת־כָּל־אֲשֶׁ֣ר נַעֲשָׂ֔ה וַיִּקְרַ֤ע מָרְדֳּכַי֙ אֶת־בְּגָדָ֔יו וַיִּלְבַּ֥שׁ שַׂ֖ק וָאֵ֑פֶר וַיֵּצֵא֙ בְּת֣וֹךְ הָעִ֔יר וַיִּזְעַ֛ק זְעָקָ֥ה גְדוֹלָ֖ה וּמָרָֽה׃ וַיָּב֕וֹא עַ֖ד לִפְנֵ֣י שַֽׁעַר־הַמֶּ֑לֶךְ כִּ֣י אֵ֥ין לָב֛וֹא אֶל־שַׁ֥עַר הַמֶּ֖לֶךְ בִּלְב֥וּשׁ שָֽׂק׃ וּבְכָל־מְדִינָ֣ה וּמְדִינָ֗ה מְקוֹם֙ אֲשֶׁ֨ר דְּבַר־הַמֶּ֤לֶךְ וְדָתוֹ֙ מַגִּ֔יעַ אֵ֤בֶל גָּדוֹל֙ לַיְּהוּדִ֔ים וְצ֥וֹם וּבְכִ֖י וּמִסְפֵּ֑ד שַׂ֣ק וָאֵ֔פֶר יֻצַּ֖ע לָֽרַבִּֽים׃ וַ֠תָּבוֹאינָה נַעֲר֨וֹת אֶסְתֵּ֤ר וְסָרִיסֶ֙יהָ֙ וַיַּגִּ֣ידוּ לָ֔הּ וַתִּתְחַלְחַ֥ל הַמַּלְכָּ֖ה מְאֹ֑ד וַתִּשְׁלַ֨ח בְּגָדִ֜ים לְהַלְבִּ֣ישׁ אֶֽת־ מָרְדֳּכַ֗י וּלְהָסִ֥יר שַׂקּ֛וֹ מֵעָלָ֖יו וְלֹ֥א קִבֵּֽל׃

βασιλέως. Καὶ ἀπεστάλη διὰ βιβλιαφόρων εἰς τὴν Ἀρταξέρξου βασιλείαν, ἀφανίσαι τὸ γένος τῶν Ἰουδαίων ἐν ἡμέρᾳ μιᾷ μηνὸς δωδεκάτου, ὅς ἐστιν Ἀδάρ, καὶ διαρπάσαι τὰ ὑπάρχοντα αὐτῶν.

Τὰ δὲ ἀντίγραφα τῶν ἐπιστολῶν ἐξετίθετο κατὰ χώραν· καὶ προσετάγη πᾶσι τοῖς ἔθνεσιν ἑτοίμους εἶναι εἰς τὴν ἡμέραν ταύτην. Ἐσπεύ- δετο δὲ τὸ πρᾶγμα καὶ εἰς Σοῦσαν· ὁ δὲ βασιλεὺς καὶ Ἁμὰν ἐκωθωνίζοντο, ἐταράσσετο δὲ ἡ πόλις.

Ὁ δὲ Μαρδοχαῖος ἐπιγνοὺς τὸ συντελούμενον διέρρηξε τὰ ἱμάτια ἑαυτοῦ, κα. ἐνεδύσατο σάκκον καὶ κατεπάσατο σποδόν, καὶ ἐκπηδήσας διὰ τῆς πλατείας τῆς πόλεως ἐβόα φωνῇ μεγάλῃ Αἴρεται ἔθνος μηδὲν ἠδικηκός. Καὶ ἦλθεν ἕως τῆς πύλης τοῦ βασιλέως, καὶ ἔστη· οὐ γὰρ ἦν αὐτῷ ἐξὸν εἰσελθεῖν εἰς τὴν αὐλὴν σάκκον ἔχοντι καὶ σποδόν. Καὶ ἐν πάσῃ χώρᾳ οὗ ἐξετίθετο τὰ

clothes to Mordecai, and sent for his sackcloth, but he would not accept her wish, so Esther called for Hatach who was one of the king's chamberlains who had been appointed to wait on her. She gave him a command to ask Mordecai why he was greiving, and what he was grieving for. So Hatach went into the city and to the gate where Mordecai was [and asked him why he grieved] and Mordecai told him all that had happened to him, and of the sum of money that Haman had promised to pay to the king's treasuries if he was allowed to destroy the Hebrew people. He also gave him [Hatach] a copy of the written decree that was given at Shushan to destroy them [the Hebrew people], [and asked Hatach] to show it to Esther, and to read it to her, and then to ask her to go to the king and intercede for her people with the king.

Hatach did as he had been instructed, and told Esther the words of Mordecai. Esther gave Hatach a command to return to Mordecai to say, "All

וַתִּקְרָא אֶסְתֵּר לַהֲתָךְ מִסָּרִיסֵי הַמֶּלֶךְ
אֲשֶׁר הֶעֱמִיד לְפָנֶיהָ וַתְּצַוֵּהוּ עַל־מָרְדֳּכָי
לָדַעַת מַה־זֶּה וְעַל־מַה־זֶּה: וַיֵּצֵא הֲתָךְ
אֶל־מָרְדֳּכָי אֶל־רְחוֹב הָעִיר אֲשֶׁר לִפְנֵי
שַׁעַר־הַמֶּלֶךְ: וַיַּגֶּד־לוֹ מָרְדֳּכַי אֵת כָּל־
אֲשֶׁר קָרָהוּ וְאֵת ׀ פָּרָשַׁת הַכֶּסֶף אֲשֶׁר
אָמַר הָמָן לִשְׁקוֹל עַל־גִּנְזֵי הַמֶּלֶךְ בַּיְּהוּדִיִּים
לְאַבְּדָם: וְאֶת־פַּתְשֶׁגֶן כְּתָב־הַדָּת אֲשֶׁר־
נִתַּן בְּשׁוּשָׁן לְהַשְׁמִידָם נָתַן לוֹ לְהַרְאוֹת
אֶת־אֶסְתֵּר וּלְהַגִּיד לָהּ וּלְצַוּוֹת עָלֶיהָ
לָבוֹא אֶל־הַמֶּלֶךְ לְהִתְחַנֶּן־לוֹ וּלְבַקֵּשׁ
מִלְּפָנָיו עַל־עַמָּהּ: וַיָּבֹא הֲתָךְ וַיַּגֵּד
לְאֶסְתֵּר אֵת דִּבְרֵי מָרְדֳּכָי: וַתֹּאמֶר
אֶסְתֵּר לַהֲתָךְ וַתְּצַוֵּהוּ אֶל־מָרְדֳּכָי: כָּל־
עַבְדֵי הַמֶּלֶךְ וְעַם מְדִינוֹת הַמֶּלֶךְ יוֹדְעִים

γράμματα κραυγῇ καὶ κοπετὸς καὶ πένθος μέγα
τοῖς Ἰουδαίοις, σάκκον καὶ σποδὸν ἔστρωσαν
ἑαυτοῖς. Καὶ εἰσῆλθον αἱ ἅβραι καὶ οἱ
εὐνοῦχοι τῆς βασιλίσσης καὶ ἀνήγγειλαν
αὐτῇ· καὶ ἐταράχθη ἀκούσασα τὸ γεγονός,
καὶ ἀπέστειλε στολίσαι τὸν Μαρδοχαῖον καὶ
ἀφελέσθαι αὐτοῦ τὸν σάκκον· ὁ δὲ οὐκ ἐπείσθη.
Ἡ δὲ Ἐσθὴρ προσεκαλέσατο Ἀχραθαῖον τὸν
εὐνοῦχον αὐτῆς, ὃς παρειστήκει αὐτῇ, καὶ ἀπέστειλε
μαθεῖν αὐτῇ παρὰ τοῦ Μαρδοχαίου τὸ ἀκριβές,
[Ἐπὶ τὴν πλατείαν πρὸς τὸ βασίλεια.]
Ὁ δὲ Μαρδοχαῖος· ὑπέδειξεν αὐτῷ τὸ γεγονὸς
καὶ τὴν ἐπαγγελίαν ἣν ἐπηγγείλατο Ἀμὰν τῷ
βασιλεῖ εἰς τὴν γάζαν ταλάντων μυρίων, ἵνα
ἀπολέσῃ τοὺς Ἰουδαίους. Καὶ τὸ ἀντίγραφον
τὸ ἐν Σούσοις ἐκτεθὲν ὑπὲρ τοῦ ἀπολέσθαι αὐτοὺς
ἔδωκεν αὐτῷ δεῖξαι τῇ Ἐσθήρ· καὶ εἶπεν αὐτῷ
ἐντείλασθαι αὐτῇ εἰσελθούσῃ παραιτήσασθαι τὸν
βασιλέα καὶ ἀξιῶσαι αὐτὸν περὶ τοῦ λαοῦ, μνη-
σθεῖσα ἡμερῶν ταπεινώσεώς σου ὡς ἐτράφης ἐν
χειρί μου, διότι Ἀμὰν ὁ δευτερεύων τῷ βασιλεῖ
ἐλάλησε καθ᾿ ἡμῶν εἰς θάνατον· ἐπικάλεσαι τὸν
Κύριον καὶ λάλησον τῷ βασιλεῖ περὶ ἡμῶν, ῥῦσαι
ἡμᾶς ἐκ θανάτου. Εἰσελθὼν δὲ ὁ Ἀχραθαῖος
ἐλάλησεν αὐτῇ πάντας τοὺς λόγους τούτους.
Εἶπε δὲ Ἐσθὴρ πρὸς Ἀχραθαῖον Πορεύθητι
πρὸς Μαρδοχαῖον καὶ εἰπὸν Ὅτι τὰ ἔθνη

the king's servants, and
the people of the king's
provinces do know that
whatsoever, whether man or
woman shall come into
the king's inner court who
is not called, will according to the one law, be put
to death, except for those
whom the king shall hold
out the golden scepter to
grant that person life--
but I have not been called
to come to the king for
the past thirty days.

Hatch told Mordecai
Esther's words. Mordecai
then commanded him to
answer Esther, "Do not
think that you will be
able to escape in the [*]
royal house any morethan
the Hebrews [in the
provinces]. If you do
not speak out at this
time then there will bea
major pogrom against the
Hebrews in another place,
and you and your father's
lineage will be destroyed
(but how are we to know if
our time here is
through?).

Esther [after listen-
ing] asked her servants to
return with this message:
"Go, gather together all
of the Hebrews that are at
Shushan and fast for me,
neither eating nor drink-

אֲשֶׁר כָּל־אִישׁ וְאִשָּׁה אֲשֶׁר־יָבוֹא אֶל־
הַמֶּלֶךְ אֶל־הֶחָצֵר הַפְּנִימִית אֲשֶׁר לֹא־
יִקָּרֵא אַחַת דָּתוֹ לְהָמִית לְבַד מֵאֲשֶׁר
יוֹשִׁיט־לוֹ הַמֶּלֶךְ אֶת־שַׁרְבִיט הַזָּהָב וְחָיָה
וַאֲנִי לֹא נִקְרֵאתִי לָבוֹא אֶל־הַמֶּלֶךְ זֶה
שְׁלוֹשִׁים יוֹם: וַיַּגִּידוּ לְמָרְדֳּכַי אֵת
דִּבְרֵי אֶסְתֵּר: וַיֹּאמֶר מָרְדֳּכַי לְהָשִׁיב
אֶל־אֶסְתֵּר אַל־תְּדַמִּי בְנַפְשֵׁךְ לְהִמָּלֵט
בֵּית־הַמֶּלֶךְ מִכָּל־הַיְּהוּדִים: כִּי אִם־
הַחֲרֵשׁ תַּחֲרִישִׁי בָּעֵת הַזֹּאת רֶוַח
וְהַצָּלָה יַעֲמוֹד לַיְּהוּדִים מִמָּקוֹם אַחֵר
וְאַתְּ וּבֵית־אָבִיךְ תֹּאבֵדוּ וּמִי יוֹדֵעַ אִם־
לְעֵת כָּזֹאת הִגַּעַתְּ לַמַּלְכוּת: וַתֹּאמֶר
אֶסְתֵּר לְהָשִׁיב אֶל־מָרְדֳּכָי: לֵךְ כְּנוֹס
אֶת־כָּל־הַיְּהוּדִים הַנִּמְצְאִים בְּשׁוּשָׁן וְצוּמוּ
עָלַי וְאַל־תֹּאכְלוּ וְאַל־תִּשְׁתּוּ שְׁלֹשֶׁת
יָמִים לַיְלָה וָיוֹם גַּם־אֲנִי וְנַעֲרֹתַי אָצוּם

πάντα τῆς βασιλείας γινώσκει, ὅτι πᾶς ἄνθρωπος
ἢ γυνὴ ὃς εἰσελεύσεται πρὸς τὸν βασιλέα εἰς τὴν
αὐλὴν τὴν ἐσωτέραν ἄκλητος, οὐκ ἔστιν αὐτῷ
σωτηρία· πλὴν ᾧ ἐκτείνῃ ὁ βασιλεὺς τὴν χρυσῆν
ῥάβδον, οὗτος σωθήσεται· κἀγὼ οὐ κέκλημαι
εἰσελθεῖν πρὸς τὸν βασιλέα, εἰσὶν αὗται ἡμέραι
τριάκοντα. Καὶ ἀπήγγειλεν Ἀχραθαῖος Μαρδοχαίῳ πάντας τοὺς λόγους Ἐσθήρ. Καὶ
εἶπε Μαρδοχαῖος πρὸς Ἀχραθαῖον Πορεύθητι καὶ
εἰπὸν αὐτῇ Ἐσθήρ, μὴ εἴπῃς σεαυτῇ ὅτι σωθήσῃ
μόνη ἐν τῇ βασιλείᾳ παρὰ πάντας τοὺς Ἰουδαίους·
Ὡς ὅτι ἐὰν παρακούσῃς ἐν τούτῳ τῷ καιρῷ,
ἄλλοθεν βοήθεια καὶ σκέπη ἔσται τοῖς Ἰουδαίοις.
Σὺ δὲ καὶ ὁ οἶκος τοῦ πατρός σου ἀπολεῖσθε·
καὶ τίς εἶδεν εἰ εἰς τὸν καιρὸν τοῦτον ἐβασίλευσας;
Καὶ ἐξαπέστειλεν Ἐσθὴρ τὸν ἥκοντα πρὸς
αὐτὴν πρὸς Μαρδοχαῖον λέγουσα Βαδίσας
ἐκκλησίασον τοὺς Ἰουδαίους τοὺς ἐν Σούσοις, καὶ
νηστεύσατε ἐπ᾽ ἐμοί, καὶ μὴ φάγητε μηδὲ πίητε
ἐπὶ ἡμέρας τρεῖς νύκτα καὶ ἡμέραν· κἀγὼ δὲ καὶ
αἱ ἅβραι μου ἀσιτήσομεν· καὶ τότε εἰσελεύσομαι

ing for three days and
nights. My maids and I
will do the same, and then
I will go to the king even
though it is against [*custom defined / tradition / royal*]
the law. If I must die, I
will die.

   Three days later,
Esther put on her royal
apparel, and stood in the
king's courtyard by his
house. The king sat on
his royal throne in the
palace, near the gate of
the house.

   When the king saw
Esther, his queen, stand-
ing in the court, she was
accepted, finding favor
with the king's eye; he
held out to her the golden
scepter that was in his
hand. Esther drew near
and touched the top

of it. The king then
asked, "What do you want,
Queen Esther? It shall be
given to you even if it is
one-half of my kingdom."

   Esther replied, "If it
seems good to the king,
let the king and Haman
come this day to a banquet
which I have prepared."

   The king ordered [a
court person] "Cause Haman
to make haste, that he may
do as Esther has asked."

   The king and Haman

כֵּן וּבְכֵן אָבוֹא אֶל־הַמֶּלֶךְ אֲשֶׁר לֹא־כַדָּת
וְכַאֲשֶׁר אָבַדְתִּי אָבָדְתִּי : וַיַּעֲבֹר מָרְדֳּכָי
וַיַּעַשׂ כְּכֹל אֲשֶׁר־צִוְּתָה עָלָיו אֶסְתֵּר :
וַיְהִי ׀ בַּיּוֹם הַשְּׁלִישִׁי וַתִּלְבַּשׁ אֶסְתֵּר
מַלְכוּת וַתַּעֲמֹד בַּחֲצַר בֵּית־הַמֶּלֶךְ הַפְּנִימִית
נֹכַח בֵּית הַמֶּלֶךְ וְהַמֶּלֶךְ יוֹשֵׁב עַל־כִּסֵּא
מַלְכוּתוֹ בְּבֵית הַמַּלְכוּת נֹכַח פֶּתַח הַבָּיִת :
וַיְהִי כִרְאוֹת הַמֶּלֶךְ אֶת־אֶסְתֵּר הַמַּלְכָּה
עֹמֶדֶת בֶּחָצֵר נָשְׂאָה חֵן בְּעֵינָיו וַיּוֹשֶׁט
הַמֶּלֶךְ לְאֶסְתֵּר אֶת־שַׁרְבִיט הַזָּהָב
אֲשֶׁר בְּיָדוֹ וַתִּקְרַב אֶסְתֵּר וַתִּגַּע בְּרֹאשׁ
הַשַּׁרְבִיט : וַיֹּאמֶר לָהּ הַמֶּלֶךְ מַה־לָּךְ
אֶסְתֵּר הַמַּלְכָּה וּמַה־בַּקָּשָׁתֵךְ עַד־חֲצִי
הַמַּלְכוּת וְיִנָּתֵן לָךְ : וַתֹּאמֶר אֶסְתֵּר
אִם־עַל־הַמֶּלֶךְ טוֹב יָבוֹא הַמֶּלֶךְ וְהָמָן
הַיּוֹם אֶל־הַמִּשְׁתֶּה אֲשֶׁר־עָשִׂיתִי לוֹ :
וַיֹּאמֶר הַמֶּלֶךְ מַהֲרוּ אֶת־הָמָן לַעֲשׂוֹת
אֶת־דְּבַר אֶסְתֵּר וַיָּבֹא הַמֶּלֶךְ וְהָמָן

πρὸς τὸν βασιλέα παρὰ τὸν νόμον, ἐὰν καὶ
ἀπολέσθαι με δέῃ.   Καὶ βαδίσας Μαρδοχαῖος
ἐποίησεν ὅσα ἐνετείλατο αὐτῷ Ἐσθήρ·
   [ΚΑΙ ἐγένετο, ἐν τῇ ἡμέρᾳ τῇ τρίτῃ
ἐνεδύσατο ἡ Ἐσθὴρ βασιλικοῖς, καὶ ἔστη ἐν αὐλῇ
τοῦ οἴκου βασιλέως τῇ ἐσωτέρα ἐξεναντίας τῆς
βασιλικῆς τοῦ βασιλέως. Ὁ δὲ βασιλεὺς ἐκάθετο
ἐν θρόνῳ τῆς ἑαυτοῦ βασιλείας ἐν τῷ
οἴκῳ βασιλικῷ ἐξεναντίας τῆς θύρας τοῦ οἴκου.
Ὡς δὲ εἶδεν ὁ βασιλεὺς Ἐσθὴρ τὴν βασίλισσαν
ἱσταμένην ἐν τῇ αὐλῇ, εὗρεν δὲ χάριν ἐν ὀφθαλ-
μοῖς αὐτοῦ, καὶ ἐκτείνας ὁ βασιλεὺς τῇ Ἐσθὴρ
τὴν ῥάβδον τὴν χρυσῆν τὴν ἐν τῇ χειρὶ αὐτοῦ,
καὶ προσῆλθεν ἡ Ἐσθὴρ καὶ ἥψατο τῆς ἄκρας
τῆς ῥάβδου.]   Καὶ εἶπεν ὁ βασιλεὺς Τί θέλεις,
Ἐσθήρ; καὶ τί σού ἐστι τὸ ἀξίωμα; ἕως τοῦ
ἡμίσους τῆς βασιλείας μου, καὶ ἔσται σοι.   Εἶπε
δὲ Ἐσθὴρ Ἡμέρα μου ἐπίσημος σήμερόν ἐστιν·
εἰ οὖν δοκεῖ τῷ βασιλεῖ, ἐλθάτω καὶ αὐτὸς καὶ
Ἀμὰν εἰς τὴν δοχὴν ἣν ποιήσω σήμερον.   Καὶ
εἶπεν ὁ βασιλεὺς Κατασπεύσατε Ἀμὰν ὅπως
ποιήσωμεν τὸν λόγον Ἐσθήρ· καὶ παραγίνονται
ἀμφότεροι εἰς τὴν δοχὴν ἣν εἶπεν Ἐσθήρ.   Ἐν

then went to the banquet which Esther had prepared [for them].

During the serving of the Banquet of Wine the king asked Esther, "What is your petition? It will be granted to you. What is your request? You shall have it to one-half of my kingdom."

Esther replied, "My petition and my request is, if I have found favor in the king's sight, and if it pleases the king to grant my petition, and to perform my request, let the king and Haman come to the banquet that I shall prepare for them, and I will do tomorrow as the king has asked."

Haman left happy and contented. But when Haman saw Mordecai in the king's gateway, and saw that he did not stand up,- nor moved when he came by he was full of hatred against Mordecai. Still Haman controlled himself.

Returning home, he called for his friends and sent for his wife Zeresh. Haman told them of the extent of his riches, the multitude of his children, all of the promotions he had received from the

אֶל־הַמִּשְׁתֶּה אֲשֶׁר־עָשְׂתָה אֶסְתֵּר: וַיֹּאמֶר
הַמֶּלֶךְ לְאֶסְתֵּר בְּמִשְׁתֵּה הַיַּיִן מַה־שְּׁאֵלָתֵךְ
וְיִנָּתֵן לָךְ וּמַה־בַּקָּשָׁתֵךְ עַד־חֲצִי הַמַּלְכוּת
וְתֵעָשׂ: וַתַּעַן אֶסְתֵּר וַתֹּאמַר שְׁאֵלָתִי
וּבַקָּשָׁתִי: אִם־מָצָאתִי חֵן בְּעֵינֵי הַמֶּלֶךְ
וְאִם־עַל־הַמֶּלֶךְ טוֹב לָתֵת אֶת־שְׁאֵלָתִי
וְלַעֲשׂוֹת אֶת־בַּקָּשָׁתִי יָבוֹא הַמֶּלֶךְ וְהָמָן
אֶל־הַמִּשְׁתֶּה אֲשֶׁר אֶעֱשֶׂה לָהֶם וּמָחָר
אֶעֱשֶׂה כִּדְבַר הַמֶּלֶךְ: וַיֵּצֵא הָמָן
בַּיּוֹם הַהוּא שָׂמֵחַ וְטוֹב לֵב וְכִרְאוֹת
הָמָן אֶת־מָרְדֳּכַי בְּשַׁעַר הַמֶּלֶךְ וְלֹא
קָם וְלֹא־זָע מִמֶּנּוּ וַיִּמָּלֵא הָמָן עַל־מָרְדֳּכַי
חֵמָה: וַיִּתְאַפַּק הָמָן וַיָּבוֹא אֶל־בֵּיתוֹ
וַיִּשְׁלַח וַיָּבֵא אֶת־אֹהֲבָיו וְאֶת־זֶרֶשׁ אִשְׁתּוֹ:
וַיְסַפֵּר לָהֶם הָמָן אֶת־כְּבוֹד עָשְׁרוֹ
וְרֹב בָּנָיו וְאֵת כָּל־אֲשֶׁר גִּדְּלוֹ הַמֶּלֶךְ
וְאֵת אֲשֶׁר נִשְּׂאוֹ עַל־הַשָּׂרִים וְעַבְדֵי

δὲ τῷ πότῳ εἶπεν ὁ βασιλεὺς πρὸς Ἐσθήρ Τί
ἐστιν, βασίλισσα Ἐσθήρ; καὶ ἔσται ὅσα ἀξιοῖς.
Καὶ εἶπε Τὸ αἴτημά μου καὶ τὸ ἀξίωμα· Εἰ
εὗρον χάριν ἐνώπιον τοῦ βασιλέως, ἐλθάτω ὁ
βασιλεὺς καὶ Ἀμὰν ἔτι τὴν αὔριον εἰς τὴν δοχὴν
ἣν ποιήσω αὐτοῖς, καὶ αὔριον ποιήσω τὰ αὐτά.
Καὶ ἐξῆλθεν ὁ Ἀμὰν ἀπὸ τοῦ βασιλέως ὑπερ-
χαρὴς εὐφραινόμενος· ἐν δὲ τῷ ἰδεῖν Ἀμὰν
Μαρδοχαῖον τὸν Ἰουδαῖον ἐν τῇ αὐλῇ ἐθυμώθη
σφόδρα. Καὶ εἰσελθὼν εἰς τὰ ἴδια ἐκάλεσε
τοὺς φίλους καὶ Ζωσάραν τὴν γυναῖκα αὐτοῦ,
Καὶ ὑπέδειξεν αὐτοῖς τὸν πλοῦτον αὐτοῦ καὶ
τὴν δόξαν ἣν ὁ βασιλεὺς αὐτῷ περιέθηκε, καὶ ὡς
ἐποίησεν αὐτὸν πρωτεύειν καὶ ἡγεῖσθαι τῆς βασι-

king, and how he had advanced above the [other] princes and other servant counsellors of the king.

Haman furthermore said, "Yes, Queen Esther invited no other man to her banquet which she had prepared but me; and tomorrow I am invited to go with the king by her invitation, again. Yet all of this is useless as long as I see Mordecai the Hebrew sitting at the king's gate."

Zeresh and all of his friends then said, "Let a gallows be made fifty cubits [7' - 10'] high, and tomorrow speak to the king that Mordecai may behanged from it, then go and enjoy the banquet with the king." Haman was pleased with their advise and had the gallows built.

That night the king could not sleep. He commanded that the book of the records of chronicles be brought to him. [When it came his servants" read to him. In it they found written that Mordecai had told of Bigthana and Teresh, two of the king's chamberlains (the keepers of the door) who had desired to overthrow the

הַמֶּלֶךְ : וַיֹּאמֶר הָמָן אַף לֹא־הֵבִיאָה
אֶסְתֵּר הַמַּלְכָּה עִם־הַמֶּלֶךְ אֶל־הַמִּשְׁתֶּה
אֲשֶׁר־עָשָׂתָה כִּי אִם־אוֹתִי וְגַם־לְמָחָר
אֲנִי קָרוּא־לָהּ עִם־הַמֶּלֶךְ : וְכָל־זֶה
אֵינֶנּוּ שֹׁוֶה לִי בְּכָל־עֵת אֲשֶׁר אֲנִי רֹאֶה
אֶת־מָרְדֳּכַי הַיְּהוּדִי יוֹשֵׁב בְּשַׁעַר הַמֶּלֶךְ :
וַתֹּאמֶר לוֹ זֶרֶשׁ אִשְׁתּוֹ וְכָל־אֹהֲבָיו
יַעֲשׂוּ־עֵץ גָּבֹהַּ חֲמִשִּׁים אַמָּה וּבַבֹּקֶר ׀
אֱמֹר לַמֶּלֶךְ וְיִתְלוּ אֶת־מָרְדֳּכַי עָלָיו
וּבֹא עִם־הַמֶּלֶךְ אֶל־הַמִּשְׁתֶּה שָׂמֵחַ וַיִּיטַב
הַדָּבָר לִפְנֵי הָמָן יִגַּעַשׂ הָעֵץ :

בַּלַּיְלָה הַהוּא נָדְדָה שְׁנַת הַמֶּלֶךְ
וַיֹּאמֶר לְהָבִיא אֶת־סֵפֶר הַזִּכְרֹנוֹת דִּבְרֵי
הַיָּמִים וַיִּהְיוּ נִקְרָאִים לִפְנֵי הַמֶּלֶךְ :
וַיִּמָּצֵא כָתוּב אֲשֶׁר הִגִּיד מָרְדֳּכַי עַל־
בִּגְתָנָא וָתֶרֶשׁ שְׁנֵי סָרִיסֵי הַמֶּלֶךְ מִשֹּׁמְרֵי
הַסַּף אֲשֶׁר בִּקְשׁוּ לִשְׁלֹחַ יָד בַּמֶּלֶךְ

λείας. Καὶ εἶπεν Ἀμάν Οὐ κέκληκεν ἡ βασίλισσα μετὰ τοῦ βασιλέως οὐδένα εἰς τὴν δοχὴν
ἀλλ' ἢ ἐμέ, καὶ εἰς τὴν αὔριον κέκλημαι. Καὶ
ταῦτά μοι οὐκ ἀρέσκει, ὅταν ἴδω Μαρδοχαῖον τὸν
Ἰουδαῖον ἐν τῇ αὐλῇ. Καὶ εἶπε πρὸς αὐτὸν
Ζωσάρα ἡ γυνὴ αὐτοῦ καὶ οἱ φίλοι Κοπήτω σοι
ξύλον πηχῶν πεντήκοντα, ὄρθρου δὲ εἰπὸν τῷ
βασιλεῖ καὶ κρεμασθήτω Μαρδοχαῖος ἐπὶ τοῦ
ξύλου· σὺ δὲ εἴσελθε εἰς τὴν δοχὴν σὺν τῷ
βασιλεῖ καὶ εὐφραίνου. Καὶ ἤρεσε τὸ ῥῆμα τῷ
Ἀμάν, καὶ ἡτοιμάσθη τὸ ξύλον.

Ὁ δὲ Κύριος ἀπέστησε τὸν ὕπνον ἀπὸ τοῦ
βασιλέως τὴν νύκτα ἐκείνην, καὶ εἶπε τῷ διακόνῳ
αὐτοῦ εἰσφέρειν γράμματα μνημόσυνα τῶν ἡμερῶν
ἀναγινώσκειν αὐτῷ. Εὗρε δὲ τὰ γράμματα τὰ
γραφέντα περὶ Μαρδοχαίου, ὡς ἀπήγγειλε τῷ
βασιλεῖ περὶ τῶν δύο εὐνούχων τοῦ βασιλέως ἐν
τῷ φυλάσσειν αὐτοὺς καὶ ζητῆσαι ἐπιβαλεῖν τὰς
χεῖρας Ἀρταξέρξῃ. Εἶπε δὲ ὁ βασιλεὺς Τίνα

king Ahasuerus. The king then said, "What honor and dignity have we given to Mordecai?" The ministers replied that nothing had been done [to date] for him.

Then the king asked, "Who is in the court?" (Now Haman was come into the outward court of the king's house to speak to the king to hang Mordecai on the gallows which he had prepared for him.)

And the king's servants replied, "Look, Haman now stands in the court." The king said, "Let him come in."

Haman came in and the king asked, "What should be done to a man the king wishes to show honor?" (Haman thought in his heart, 'Who other than myself would the king wish to honor?') Haman answered the king, "The man that the king wishes to honor should be brought royal clothing that the king used to wear, and he should be given a horse that the king used to ride, and there should be a royal crown set upon his head.

"And, let this apparel and horse be delivered to

אֲחַשְׁוֵרוֹשׁ: וַיֹּאמֶר הַמֶּלֶךְ מַה־נַּעֲשָׂה
יְקָר וּגְדוּלָּה לְמָרְדֳּכַי עַל־זֶה וַיֹּאמְרוּ נַעֲרֵי
הַמֶּלֶךְ מְשָׁרְתָיו לֹא־נַעֲשָׂה עִמּוֹ דָּבָר:
וַיֹּאמֶר הַמֶּלֶךְ מִי בֶחָצֵר וְהָמָן בָּא לַחֲצַר
בֵּית־הַמֶּלֶךְ הַחִיצוֹנָה לֵאמֹר לַמֶּלֶךְ
לִתְלוֹת אֶת־מָרְדֳּכַי עַל־הָעֵץ אֲשֶׁר־הֵכִין
לוֹ: וַיֹּאמְרוּ נַעֲרֵי הַמֶּלֶךְ אֵלָיו הִנֵּה
הָמָן עֹמֵד בֶּחָצֵר וַיֹּאמֶר הַמֶּלֶךְ יָבוֹא:
וַיָּבוֹא הָמָן וַיֹּאמֶר לוֹ הַמֶּלֶךְ מַה־לַעֲשׂוֹת
בָּאִישׁ אֲשֶׁר הַמֶּלֶךְ חָפֵץ בִּיקָרוֹ וַיֹּאמֶר
הָמָן בְּלִבּוֹ לְמִי יַחְפֹּץ הַמֶּלֶךְ לַעֲשׂוֹת
יְקָר יוֹתֵר מִמֶּנִּי: וַיֹּאמֶר הָמָן אֶל־הַמֶּלֶךְ
אִישׁ אֲשֶׁר הַמֶּלֶךְ חָפֵץ בִּיקָרוֹ: יָבִיאוּ
לְבוּשׁ מַלְכוּת אֲשֶׁר לָבַשׁ־בּוֹ הַמֶּלֶךְ וְסוּס
אֲשֶׁר רָכַב עָלָיו הַמֶּלֶךְ וַאֲשֶׁר נִתַּן כֶּתֶר
מַלְכוּת בְּרֹאשׁוֹ: וְנָתוֹן הַלְּבוּשׁ וְהַסּוּס
עַל־יַד־אִישׁ מִשָּׂרֵי הַמֶּלֶךְ הַפַּרְתְּמִים

δόξαν ἢ χάριν ἐποιήσαμεν τῷ Μαρδοχαίῳ; καὶ εἶπαν οἱ διάκονοι τοῦ βασιλέως Οὐκ ἐποίησας αὐτῷ οὐδέν. Ἐν δὲ τῷ πυνθάνεσθαι τὸν βασιλέα περὶ τῆς εὐνοίας Μαρδοχαίου, ἰδοὺ Ἀμὰν ἐν τῇ αὐλῇ· εἶπε δὲ ὁ βασιλεύς Τίς ἐν τῇ αὐλῇ; ὁ δὲ Ἀμὰν εἰσῆλθεν εἰπεῖν τῷ βασιλεῖ κρεμάσαι τὸν Μαρδοχαῖον ἐπὶ τῷ ξύλῳ ᾧ ἡτοίμασε. Καὶ εἶπαν οἱ διάκονοι τοῦ βασιλέως Ἰδοὺ Ἀμὰν ἕστηκεν ἐν τῇ αὐλῇ· καὶ εἶπεν ὁ βασιλεύς Καλέσατε αὐτόν. Εἶπε δὲ ὁ βασιλεὺς τῷ Ἀμάν Τί ποιήσω τῷ ἀνθρώπῳ ὃν ἐγὼ θέλω δοξάσαι; εἶπε δὲ ἐν ἑαυτῷ Ἀμάν Τίνα θέλει ὁ βασιλεὺς δοξάσαι εἰ μὴ ἐμέ; Εἶπε δὲ πρὸς τὸν βασιλέα Ἄνθρωπον ὃν ὁ βασιλεὺς θέλει δοξάσαι, Ἐνεγκάτωσαν οἱ παῖδες τοῦ βασιλέως στολὴν βυσσίνην ἣν ὁ βασιλεὺς περιβάλλεται, καὶ ἵππον ἐφ᾽ ὃν ὁ βασιλεὺς ἐπιβαίνει, Καὶ δότω ἑνὶ τῶν φίλων τοῦ βασιλέως τῶν ἐνδόξων καὶ στολισάτω τὸν ἀνθρω-

the hand of one of the king's most noble princes that they may array the man with everything whom the king wishes to honor, and then bring him on horseback through the street of the city, proclaiming before him, "This is what shall be done to the man the king wishes to honor."

The king then said to Haman, "Make haste, and take the apparel and the horse as you have said, and so to Mordecai the Hebrew that sits at the king's gateway. Make sure that you do everything as you have said."

Haman took the apparel and the horse as the king ordered and arrayed Mordecai, and brought him on horseback through the city streets, proclaiming "This is what shall be done to the man that the king wishes to honor."

Mordecai came again to the king's gate, but Haman returned to his own house mourning, having his head covered. Haman told his wife Zeresh and all of his friends everything that had befallen him. But the men he trusted for

וְהִלְבִּשׁוּ אֶת־הָאִישׁ אֲשֶׁר הַמֶּלֶךְ חָפֵץ
בִּיקָרוֹ וְהִרְכִּיבֻהוּ עַל־הַסּוּס בִּרְחוֹב הָעִיר
וְקָרְאוּ לְפָנָיו כָּכָה יֵעָשֶׂה לָאִישׁ אֲשֶׁר
הַמֶּלֶךְ חָפֵץ בִּיקָרוֹ: וַיֹּאמֶר הַמֶּלֶךְ
לְהָמָן מַהֵר קַח אֶת־הַלְּבוּשׁ וְאֶת־הַסּוּס
כַּאֲשֶׁר דִּבַּרְתָּ וַעֲשֵׂה־כֵן לְמָרְדֳּכַי הַיְּהוּדִי
הַיּוֹשֵׁב בְּשַׁעַר הַמֶּלֶךְ אַל־תַּפֵּל דָּבָר מִכֹּל
אֲשֶׁר דִּבַּרְתָּ: וַיִּקַּח הָמָן אֶת־הַלְּבוּשׁ וְאֶת־
הַסּוּס וַיַּלְבֵּשׁ אֶת־מָרְדֳּכַי וַיַּרְכִּיבֵהוּ בִּרְחוֹב
הָעִיר וַיִּקְרָא לְפָנָיו כָּכָה יֵעָשֶׂה לָאִישׁ
אֲשֶׁר הַמֶּלֶךְ חָפֵץ בִּיקָרוֹ: וַיָּשָׁב מָרְדֳּכַי
אֶל־שַׁעַר הַמֶּלֶךְ וְהָמָן נִדְחַף אֶל־בֵּיתוֹ
אָבֵל וַחֲפוּי רֹאשׁ: וַיְסַפֵּר הָמָן לְזֶרֶשׁ
אִשְׁתּוֹ וּלְכָל־אֹהֲבָיו אֵת כָּל־אֲשֶׁר קָרָהוּ
וַיֹּאמְרוּ לוֹ חֲכָמָיו וְזֶרֶשׁ אִשְׁתּוֹ אִם מִזֶּרַע
הַיְּהוּדִים מָרְדֳּכַי אֲשֶׁר הַחִלּוֹתָ לִנְפֹּל
לְפָנָיו לֹא־תוּכַל לוֹ כִּי־נָפוֹל תִּפּוֹל לְפָנָיו:

πον ὃν ὁ βασιλεὺς ἀγαπᾷ, καὶ ἀναβιβασάτω αὐτὸν ἐπὶ τὸν ἵππον, καὶ κηρυσσέτω διὰ τῆς πλατείας τῆς πόλεως λέγων Οὕτως ἔσται παντὶ ἀνθρώπῳ ὃν ὁ βασιλεὺς δοξάζει. Εἶπε δὲ ὁ βασιλεὺς τῷ Ἀμάν Καλῶς ἐλάλησας· οὕτως ποίησον τῷ Μαρδοχαίῳ τῷ Ἰουδαίῳ τῷ θεραπεύοντι ἐν τῇ αὐλῇ, καὶ μὴ παραπεσάτω σου λόγος ὧν ἐλάλησας. Ἔλαβε δὲ Ἀμάν τὴν στολὴν καὶ τὸν ἵππον, καὶ ἐστόλισε τὸν Μαρδοχαῖον καὶ ἀνεβίβασεν αὐτὸν ἐπὶ τὸν ἵππον, καὶ διῆλθε διὰ τῆς πλατείας τῆς πόλεως καὶ ἐκήρυσσε λέγων Οὕτως ἔσται παντὶ ἀνθρώπῳ ὃν ὁ βασιλεὺς θέλει δοξάσαι. Ἐπέστρεψε δὲ ὁ Μαρδοχαῖος εἰς τὴν αὐλήν· Ἀμὰν δὲ ὑπέστρεψεν εἰς τὰ ἴδια λυπούμενος κατὰ κεφαλῆς. Καὶ διηγήσατο Ἀμὰν τὰ συμβεβηκότα αὐτῷ Ζωσάρᾳ τῇ γυναικὶ αὐτοῦ καὶ τοῖς φίλοις· καὶ εἶπαν πρὸς αὐτὸν οἱ φίλοι καὶ ἡ γυνὴ Εἰ ἐκ γένους Ἰουδαίων Μαρδοχαῖος, ἤρξαι ταπεινοῦσθαι ἐνώπιον· αὐτοῦ, πεσὼν πεσῇ, καὶ οὐ μὴ δύνῃ αὐτὸν ἀμύνασθαι, ὅτι θεὸς ζῶν μετ' αὐτοῦ.

counsel, and his wife, said, "If Mordecai be of the seed of the Jews, before whom you have begun to fall, you will not win against him, but you will fall beneath him." While they were talking the king's chamberlain came to hurry Haman to the banquet Esther had prepared.

The king and Haman came to the banquet of Queen Esther. And, on the second day of the Banquet of Wine, the king asked, of Esther, "What is your petition, Queen Esther? Ask and it shall be granted. What is your request? It 'shall be performed, even to one-half of my kingdom."

Esther replied, "If I have found favor in your sight, my King, and if it pleases the king, let my life be given me at my petition, and my people at my request, for we are sold, and I and my people are to be destroyed, to be slain, and to perish.

"But if we had been sold for bondmen and bondswomen, I would have held my tongue eventhough the enemy could not countervail the king's damage."

עוֹדָם מְדַבְּרִים עִמּוֹ וְסָרִיסֵי הַמֶּלֶךְ הִגִּיעוּ וַיַּבְהִלוּ לְהָבִיא אֶת־הָמָן אֶל־הַמִּשְׁתֶּה אֲשֶׁר־עָשְׂתָה אֶסְתֵּר :
וַיָּבֹא הַמֶּלֶךְ וְהָמָן לִשְׁתּוֹת עִם־אֶסְתֵּר הַמַּלְכָּה : וַיֹּאמֶר הַמֶּלֶךְ לְאֶסְתֵּר גַּם בַּיּוֹם הַשֵּׁנִי בְּמִשְׁתֵּה הַיַּיִן מַה־שְּׁאֵלָתֵךְ אֶסְתֵּר הַמַּלְכָּה וְתִנָּתֵן לָךְ וּמַה־בַּקָּשָׁתֵךְ עַד־חֲצִי הַמַּלְכוּת וְתֵעָשׂ : וַתַּעַן אֶסְתֵּר הַמַּלְכָּה וַתֹּאמַר אִם־מָצָאתִי חֵן בְּעֵינֶיךָ הַמֶּלֶךְ וְאִם־עַל־הַמֶּלֶךְ טוֹב תִּנָּתֶן־לִי נַפְשִׁי בִּשְׁאֵלָתִי וְעַמִּי בְּבַקָּשָׁתִי : כִּי נִמְכַּרְנוּ אֲנִי וְעַמִּי לְהַשְׁמִיד לַהֲרוֹג וּלְאַבֵּד וְאִלּוּ לַעֲבָדִים וְלִשְׁפָחוֹת נִמְכַּרְנוּ הֶחֱרַשְׁתִּי כִּי אֵין הַצָּר שֹׁוֶה בְּנֵזֶק הַמֶּלֶךְ :

Ἔτι αὐτῶν λαλούντων παραγίνονται οἱ εὐνοῦχοι ἐπισπεύδοντες τὸν Ἀμὰν ἐπὶ τὸν πότον ὃν ἡτοί·μασεν Ἐσθήρ.

ΕΙΣΗΛΘΕ δὲ ὁ βασιλεὺς καὶ Ἀμὰν συμπιεῖν τῇ βασιλίσσῃ. Εἶπε δὲ ὁ βασιλεὺς Ἐσθὴρ τῇ δευτέρᾳ ἡμέρᾳ ἐν τῷ πότῳ Τί ἐστιν, Ἐσθὴρ βασίλισσα, καὶ τί τὸ αἴτημά σου καὶ τί τὸ ἀξίωμά σου; καὶ ἔστω σοι ἕως ἡμίσους τῆς βασιλείας μου. Καὶ ἀποκριθεῖσα εἶπεν Εἰ εὗρον χάριν ἐνώπιον τοῦ βασιλέως, δοθήτω ἡ ψυχὴ τῷ αἰτήματί μου, καὶ ὁ λαός μου τῷ ἀξιώματί μου. Ἐπράθημεν γὰρ ἐγώ τε καὶ ὁ λαός μου εἰς ἀπώλειαν καὶ διαρπαγὴν καὶ δουλείαν, ἡμεῖς καὶ τὰ τέκνα ἡμῶν εἰς παῖδας καὶ παιδίσκας, καὶ παρήκουσα· οὐ γὰρ ἄξιος ὁ διάβολος τῆς αὐλῆς τοῦ βασιλέως. Εἶπε δὲ ὁ βασιλεὺς Τίς οὗτος

King Ahasuerus replied to Queen Esther, "Who is he, and where is he, that did presume in his heart to do such a thing? [as you tell me]"

Esther answered, "The adversary and enemy is the wicked Haman." (Then Haman trembled before the king and queen.)

The king, rising from the Banquet of Wine, was angry and went into the palace garden. Haman stood up to request that his life be spared, petioning Queen Esther, for he realized that the king meant to do him harm.

The king returned out of the garden into the place of the Banquet of Wine to find Haman had fallen upon the same bed as where Esther was. The king questioned, "Will he rape the Queen also in front of me in my own house?" As the word came from the king's mouth they [the king's chamberlains] covered Haman's face. Harbonah, one of the chamberlains, said to the king, "Look at the fifty cubits gallows Haman has had built for Mordecai who had spoken good things for the king; they

וַיֹּאמֶר הַמֶּלֶךְ אֲחַשְׁוֵרוֹשׁ וַיֹּאמֶר לְאֶסְתֵּר הַמַּלְכָּה מִי הוּא זֶה וְאֵי־זֶה הוּא אֲשֶׁר־מְלָאוֹ לִבּוֹ לַעֲשׂוֹת כֵּן: וַתֹּאמֶר אֶסְתֵּר אִישׁ צַר וְאוֹיֵב הָמָן הָרָע הַזֶּה וְהָמָן נִבְעַת מִלִּפְנֵי הַמֶּלֶךְ וְהַמַּלְכָּה: וְהַמֶּלֶךְ קָם בַּחֲמָתוֹ מִמִּשְׁתֵּה הַיַּיִן אֶל־גִּנַּת הַבִּיתָן וְהָמָן עָמַד לְבַקֵּשׁ עַל־נַפְשׁוֹ מֵאֶסְתֵּר הַמַּלְכָּה כִּי רָאָה כִּי־כָלְתָה אֵלָיו הָרָעָה מֵאֵת הַמֶּלֶךְ: וְהַמֶּלֶךְ שָׁב מִגִּנַּת הַבִּיתָן אֶל־בֵּית ׀ מִשְׁתֵּה הַיַּיִן וְהָמָן נֹפֵל עַל־הַמִּטָּה אֲשֶׁר אֶסְתֵּר עָלֶיהָ וַיֹּאמֶר הַמֶּלֶךְ הֲגַם לִכְבּוֹשׁ אֶת־הַמַּלְכָּה עִמִּי בַּבָּיִת הַדָּבָר יָצָא מִפִּי הַמֶּלֶךְ וּפְנֵי הָמָן חָפוּ: וַיֹּאמֶר חַרְבוֹנָה אֶחָד מִן־הַסָּרִיסִים לִפְנֵי הַמֶּלֶךְ גַּם הִנֵּה־הָעֵץ אֲשֶׁר־עָשָׂה

ὅστις ἐτόλμησε ποιῆσαι τὸ πρᾶγμα τοῦτο; Εἶπε δὲ Ἐσθήρ Ἄνθρωπος ἐχθρὸς Ἀμὰν ὁ πονηρὸς οὗτος. Ἀμὰν δὲ ἐταράχθη ἀπὸ τοῦ βασιλέως καὶ τῆς βασιλίσσης. Ὁ δὲ βασιλεὺς ἐξανέστη ἀπὸ τοῦ συμποσίου εἰς τὸν κῆπον· ὁ δὲ Ἀμὰν παρῃτεῖτο τὴν βασίλισσαν, ἑώρα γὰρ ἑαυτὸν ἐν κακοῖς ὄντα. Ἐπέστρεψε δὲ ὁ βασιλεὺς ἐκ τοῦ κήπου, Ἀμὰν δὲ ἐπιπεπτώκει ἐπὶ τὴν κλίνην ἀξιῶν τὴν βασίλισσαν· εἶπε δὲ ὁ βασιλεὺς Ὥστε καὶ τὴν γυναῖκα βιάζῃ ἐν τῇ οἰκίᾳ μου; Ἀμὰν δὲ ἀκούσας διετράπη τῷ προσώπῳ. Εἶπε δὲ Βουγαθὰν εἷς τῶν εὐνούχων πρὸς τὸν βασιλέα Ἰδοὺ καὶ ξύλον ἡτοίμασεν Ἀμὰν Μαρδοχαίῳ τῷ λαλήσαντι περὶ

stand in the house of Haman." The king ordered, "Hang him on them", and they hanged Haman on the gallows that he had prepared for Mordecai.

Only then was the king's wrath pacified.

That same day King Ahasuerus gave Haman's house to the Esther the queen, for Haman was the Jews enemy. Then Mordecai came before the king, for Esther revealed to the king what Mordecai was to her, and the king took off his ring, which he had taken from Haman, and gave it to Mordecai.

Esther gave Mordecai the ownership of Haman's own house, and then spoke to the king, falling down at his feet, beseeching him with her tears to end the evil plans of Haman the Agagite which was to end the life of all Jews [literarlly translates: "to end the device that he had devised against the Jews"]. The king held out the golden scepter to Esther. Esther arose and stood before the king and said, "If it pleases the king, and if I have found favor in his sight, and [if] the thing seems to be

הָמָן לְמָרְדֳּכַי אֲשֶׁר־דִּבֶּר־טוֹב עַל־הַמֶּלֶךְ עֹמֵד בְּבֵית הָמָן גָּבֹהַ חֲמִשִּׁים אַמָּה וַיֹּאמֶר הַמֶּלֶךְ תְּלֻהוּ עָלָיו: וַיִּתְלוּ אֶת־הָמָן עַל־הָעֵץ אֲשֶׁר־הֵכִין לְמָרְדֳּכָי וַחֲמַת הַמֶּלֶךְ שָׁכָכָה:

בַּיּוֹם הַהוּא נָתַן הַמֶּלֶךְ אֲחַשְׁוֵרוֹשׁ לְאֶסְתֵּר הַמַּלְכָּה אֶת־בֵּית הָמָן צֹרֵר הַיְּהוּדִיִּים וּמָרְדֳּכַי בָּא לִפְנֵי הַמֶּלֶךְ כִּי־הִגִּידָה אֶסְתֵּר מָה הוּא־לָהּ: וַיָּסַר הַמֶּלֶךְ אֶת־טַבַּעְתּוֹ אֲשֶׁר הֶעֱבִיר מֵהָמָן וַיִּתְּנָהּ לְמָרְדֳּכָי וַתָּשֶׂם אֶסְתֵּר אֶת־מָרְדֳּכַי עַל־בֵּית הָמָן: וַתּוֹסֶף אֶסְתֵּר וַתְּדַבֵּר לִפְנֵי הַמֶּלֶךְ וַתִּפֹּל לִפְנֵי רַגְלָיו וַתֵּבְךְּ וַתִּתְחַנֶּן־לוֹ לְהַעֲבִיר אֶת־רָעַת הָמָן הָאֲגָגִי וְאֵת מַחֲשַׁבְתּוֹ אֲשֶׁר חָשַׁב עַל־הַיְּהוּדִים: וַיּוֹשֶׁט הַמֶּלֶךְ לְאֶסְתֵּר אֵת שַׁרְבִט הַזָּהָב וַתָּקָם אֶסְתֵּר וַתַּעֲמֹד לִפְנֵי הַמֶּלֶךְ: וַתֹּאמֶר אִם־עַל־הַמֶּלֶךְ טוֹב וְאִם־מָצָאתִי חֵן לְפָנָיו וְכָשֵׁר

τοῦ βασιλέως, καὶ ὤρθωται ἐν τοῖς Ἀμὰν ξύλον πηχῶν πεντήκοντα. Εἶπε δὲ ὁ βασιλεὺς Σταυρωθήτω ἐπ' αὐτοῦ. Καὶ ἐκρεμάσθη Ἀμὰν ἐπὶ τοῦ ξύλου ὃ ἡτοιμάσθη Μαρδοχαίῳ. Καὶ τότε ὁ βασιλεὺς ἐκόπασε τοῦ θυμοῦ.

ΚΑΙ ἐν αὐτῇ τῇ ἡμέρᾳ ὁ βασιλεὺς Ἀρταξέρξης ἐδωρήσατο Ἐσθὴρ ὅσα ὑπῆρχεν Ἀμὰν τῷ διαβόλῳ, καὶ Μαρδοχαῖος προσεκλήθη ὑπὸ τοῦ βασιλέως· ὑπέδειξε γὰρ Ἐσθὴρ ὅτι ἐνοικείωται αὐτῇ. Ἔλαβε δὲ ὁ βασιλεὺς τὸν δακτύλιον ὃν ἀφείλατο Ἀμάν· καὶ ἔδωκεν αὐτὸν Μαρδοχαίῳ, καὶ κατέστησεν Ἐσθὴρ Μαρδοχαῖον ἐπὶ πάντων τῶν Ἀμάν. Καὶ προσθεῖσα ἐλάλησε πρὸς τὸν βασιλέα, καὶ προσέπεσε πρὸς τοὺς πόδας αὐτοῦ, καὶ ἠξίου

right before the king and,
if I am pleasing in his
sight, let it be written
to reverse the letters
devised by Haman the son
of Hammedath the Agagite,
which he wrote to destroy
the Jews which are in all
of the king's provinces;
for how can I endure to
see the evil that shall
come to my own people? Or,
how can I watch the de-
struction of my own
people?"

King Ahasuerus said
to Queen Esther and to
Mordecai the Jew, "I have
given Esther Haman's own
house, and they have hanged him on the gallows
because he laid his hands
on the Jews. Now write
as you wish concerning
the Jews, and do so using
the King's name, for what
is written in the king's
name, and is sealed with
the king's ring, no man
can reverse."

Then the king's record-
ers were called (in
the third month, that is
the month of Sivan, of
the twenty-third day, and
wrote down all things
that Mordecai commanded
the Jews [to know], and
also to the lieutenants,
and to the deputies and

הַדָּבָר לִפְנֵי הַמֶּלֶךְ וְטוֹבָה אֲנִי בְּעֵינָיו
יִכָּתֵב לְהָשִׁיב אֶת־הַסְּפָרִים מַחֲשֶׁבֶת הָמָן
בֶּן־הַמְּדָתָא הָאֲגָגִי אֲשֶׁר כָּתַב לְאַבֵּד
אֶת־הַיְּהוּדִים אֲשֶׁר בְּכָל־מְדִינוֹת הַמֶּלֶךְ :
כִּי אֵיכָכָה אוּכַל וְרָאִיתִי בָּרָעָה אֲשֶׁר־
יִמְצָא אֶת־עַמִּי וְאֵיכָכָה אוּכַל וְרָאִיתִי
בְּאָבְדַן מוֹלַדְתִּי : וַיֹּאמֶר הַמֶּלֶךְ
אֲחַשְׁוֵרֹשׁ לְאֶסְתֵּר הַמַּלְכָּה וּלְמָרְדֳּכַי
הַיְּהוּדִי הִנֵּה בֵית־הָמָן נָתַתִּי לְאֶסְתֵּר
וְאֹתוֹ תָּלוּ עַל־הָעֵץ עַל אֲשֶׁר־שָׁלַח
יָדוֹ בַּיְּהוּדִים : וְאַתֶּם כִּתְבוּ עַל־
הַיְּהוּדִים כַּטּוֹב בְּעֵינֵיכֶם בְּשֵׁם הַמֶּלֶךְ
וְחִתְמוּ בְּטַבַּעַת הַמֶּלֶךְ כִּי־כְתָב אֲשֶׁר־
נִכְתָּב בְּשֵׁם־הַמֶּלֶךְ וְנַחְתּוֹם בְּטַבַּעַת
הַמֶּלֶךְ אֵין לְהָשִׁיב : וַיִּקָּרְאוּ סֹפְרֵי־הַמֶּלֶךְ
בָּעֵת־הַהִיא בַּחֹדֶשׁ הַשְּׁלִישִׁי הוּא־חֹדֶשׁ
סִיוָן בִּשְׁלוֹשָׁה וְעֶשְׂרִים בּוֹ וַיִּכָּתֵב כְּכָל־
אֲשֶׁר־צִוָּה מָרְדֳּכַי אֶל־הַיְּהוּדִים וְאֶל
הָאֲחַשְׁדַּרְפְּנִים־וְהַפַּחוֹת וְשָׂרֵי הַמְּדִינוֹת
אֲשֶׁר מֵהֹדּוּ וְעַד־כּוּשׁ שֶׁבַע וְעֶשְׂרִים
וּמֵאָה מְדִינָה מְדִינָה וּמְדִינָה כִּכְתָבָהּ

ἀφελεῖν τὴν Ἀμὰν κακίαν καὶ ὅσα ἐποίησε τοῖς
Ἰουδαίοις. Ἐξέτεινε δὲ ὁ βασιλεὺς Ἐσθὴρ τὴν
ῥάβδον τὴν χρυσῆν· ἐξηγέρθη δὲ Ἐσθὴρ παρε-
στηκέναι τῷ βασιλεῖ. Καὶ εἶπεν Ἐσθήρ Εἰ δοκεῖ
σοι καὶ εὗρον χάριν, πεμφθήτω ἀποστραφῆναι τὰ
γράμματα τὰ ἀπεσταλμένα ὑπὸ Ἀμάν, τὰ γραφέντα ἀπολέσθαι τοὺς Ἰουδαίους οἳ εἰσιν ἐν τῇ
βασιλείᾳ σου. Πῶς γὰρ δυνήσομαι ἰδεῖν τὴν
κάκωσιν τοῦ λαοῦ μου, καὶ πῶς δυνήσομαι σωθῆναι
ἐν τῇ ἀπωλείᾳ τῆς πατρίδος μου; Καὶ εἶπεν
ὁ βασιλεὺς πρὸς Ἐσθήρ Εἰ πάντα τὰ ὑπάρχοντα
Ἀμάν ἔδωκα καὶ ἐχαρισάμην σοι, καὶ αὐτὸν

rulers of the provinces
which extend from India
to Ethiopia, being in all
one hundred and twenty-
seven provinces; to every
province [the instructions
were written] in the writing of that area, and to
every people according
to the language of the
people who lived there,
and to the Jews according
to their writing and their
language.

And he wrote it in
the king Ahasuerus name,
and sealed it with the
king's ring; and, he sent
the letters by messengers
on horseback, as well as
by riders on mules,
camels, and young dromedar-
ies.

The king granted the
Jews which were in every
city to gather together as
a community, and to defend
their life even by
destroying, slaying, or
causing to perish all the
power of the people and [the]
province that would as-
sault them, including both
women and children, and to
take the spoil of them as
booty, if it was done within one day, throughout all
of King Ahasuerus' prov-
inces, being the thir-
teenth day of the twelfth

וְעָם וָעָם כִּלְשֹׁנוֹ וְאֶל־הַיְּהוּדִים כִּכְתָבָם
וְכִלְשׁוֹנָם : וַיִּכְתֹּב בְּשֵׁם הַמֶּלֶךְ
אֲחַשְׁוֵרֹשׁ וַיַּחְתֹּם בְּטַבַּעַת הַמֶּלֶךְ וַיִּשְׁלַח
סְפָרִים בְּיַד הָרָצִים בַּסּוּסִים רֹכְבֵי
הָרֶכֶשׁ הָאֲחַשְׁתְּרָנִים בְּנֵי הָרַמָּכִים :
אֲשֶׁר נָתַן הַמֶּלֶךְ לַיְּהוּדִים ׀ אֲשֶׁר
בְּכָל־עִיר וָעִיר לְהִקָּהֵל וְלַעֲמֹד עַל־נַפְשָׁם
לְהַשְׁמִיד לַהֲרֹג וּלְאַבֵּד אֶת־כָּל־חֵיל
עַם וּמְדִינָה הַצָּרִים אֹתָם טַף וְנָשִׁים
וּשְׁלָלָם לָבוֹז : בְּיוֹם אֶחָד בְּכָל־
מְדִינוֹת הַמֶּלֶךְ אֲחַשְׁוֵרֹשׁ בִּשְׁלוֹשָׁה עָשָׂר
לְחֹדֶשׁ שְׁנֵים־עָשָׂר הוּא־חֹדֶשׁ אֲדָר :

ἐκρέμασα ἐπὶ ξύλου ὅτι τὰς χεῖρας ἐπήνεγκε τοῖς
Ἰουδαίοις, τί ἔτι ἐπιζητεῖς; Γράψατε καὶ ὑμεῖς
ἐκ τοῦ ὀνόματός μου ὡς δοκεῖ ὑμῖν, καὶ σφραγί-
σατε τῷ δακτυλίῳ μου· ὅσα γὰρ γράφεται τοῦ
βασιλέως ἐπιτάξαντος καὶ σφραγισθῇ τῷ δακτυλίῳ
μου, οὐκ ἔστιν αὐτοῖς ἀντειπεῖν. Ἐκλήθησαν
δὲ οἱ γραμματεῖς ἐν τῷ πρώτῳ μηνὶ ὅς ἐστι
Νισάν, τρίτῃ καὶ εἰκάδι τοῦ αὐτοῦ ἔτους, καὶ
ἐγράφη τοῖς Ἰουδαίοις ὅσα ἐνετείλατο τοῖς οἰκονόμοις καὶ τοῖς ἄρχουσι τῶν σατραπῶν ἀπὸ τῆς
Ἰνδικῆς ἕως τῆς Αἰθιοπίας, ἑκατὸν εἰκοσιεπτὰ
σατράπαις κατὰ χώραν καὶ χώραν, κατὰ τὴν
αὐτῶν λέξιν. Ἐγράφη δὲ διὰ τοῦ βασιλέως
καὶ ἐσφραγίσθη τῷ δακτυλίῳ αὐτοῦ, καὶ ἐξαπέ-
στειλαν τὰ γράμματα διὰ βιβλιοφόρων, Ὡς
ἐπέταξεν αὐτοῖς χρῆσθαι τοῖς νόμοις αὐτῶν
ἐν πάσῃ πόλει, βοηθῆσαί τε αὐτοῖς καὶ
χρῆσθαι τοῖς ἀντιδίκοις αὐτῶν καὶ τοῖς
ἀντικειμένοις αὐτῶν ὡς βούλονται, Ἐν
ἡμέρᾳ μιᾷ ἐν πάσῃ τῇ βασιλείᾳ Ἀρταξέρξου, τῇ

month, which is the month of Adar.

A copy of this order which was to go to every province was published for all people, and the Jews were [warned] to be ready against that day to avenge themselves on their enemies. And the couriers went out upon mules and [on] camels being hastened on their way by the command of the king. The decree was also read at the Shushan palace.

Mordecai then went out from the presence of the king wearing royal apparel of blue and white and with a great crown of gold, and with a garment of fine linen [being dyed and fashioned] of purple.

The city of Shushan rejoiced and was glad.

The Jews had light and gladness and joy, and honor, and in every province, and in every city, wherever the king's command had reached, the Jews had joy and gladness and a feast and a good day. And many of the people of the land became Jews because the fear of the Jews settled over them.

In the twelfth month,

פַּתְשֶׁגֶן הַכְּתָב לְהִנָּתֵן דָּת בְּכָל־מְדִינָה וּמְדִינָה גָּלוּי לְכָל־הָעַמִּים וְלִהְיוֹת הַיְּהוּדִיִּים עֲתוּדִים לַיּוֹם הַזֶּה לְהִנָּקֵם מֵאֹיְבֵיהֶם : הָרָצִים רֹכְבֵי הָרֶכֶשׁ הָאֲחַשְׁתְּרָנִים יָצְאוּ מְבֹהָלִים וּדְחוּפִים בִּדְבַר הַמֶּלֶךְ וְהַדָּת נִתְּנָה בְּשׁוּשַׁן הַבִּירָה : וּמָרְדֳּכַי יָצָא מִלִּפְנֵי הַמֶּלֶךְ בִּלְבוּשׁ מַלְכוּת תְּכֵלֶת וָחוּר וַעֲטֶרֶת זָהָב גְּדוֹלָה וְתַכְרִיךְ בּוּץ וְאַרְגָּמָן וְהָעִיר שׁוּשָׁן צָהֲלָה וְשָׂמֵחָה : לַיְּהוּדִים הָיְתָה אוֹרָה וְשִׂמְחָה וְשָׂשֹׂן וִיקָר : וּבְכָל־ מְדִינָה וּמְדִינָה וּבְכָל־עִיר וָעִיר מְקוֹם אֲשֶׁר דְּבַר־הַמֶּלֶךְ וְדָתוֹ מַגִּיעַ שִׂמְחָה וְשָׂשׂוֹן לַיְּהוּדִים מִשְׁתֶּה וְיוֹם טוֹב וְרַבִּים מֵעַמֵּי הָאָרֶץ מִתְיַהֲדִים כִּי־נָפַל פַּחַד־ הַיְּהוּדִים עֲלֵיהֶם :
וּבִשְׁנֵים עָשָׂר חֹדֶשׁ הוּא־חֹדֶשׁ אֲדָר

τρισκαιδεκάτῃ τοῦ δωδεκάτου μηνὸς ὅς ἐστιν Ἀδάρ.

Ὧν ἐστιν ἀντίγραφον τῆς ἐπιστολῆς τὰ ὑπο-γεγραμμένα. [Τὰ δὲ ἀντίγραφα ἐκτεθείσθω ὀφθαλμοφανῶς ἐν πάσῃ τῇ βασιλείᾳ, ἑτοίμους δὲ εἶναι πάντας τοὺς Ἰουδαίους εἰς ταύτην τὴν ἡμέραν, πολεμῆσαι αὐτῶν τοὺς ὑπεναντίους.] Οἱ μὲν οὖν ἱππεῖς ἐξῆλθον σπεύδοντες τὰ ὑπὸ τοῦ βασιλέως λεγόμενα ἐπιτελεῖν· ἐξετέθη δὲ τὸ πρόσταγμα καὶ ἐν Σούσοις. Ὁ δὲ Μαρδοχαῖος ἐξῆλθεν ἐστολισμένος τὴν βασιλικὴν στολὴν καὶ στέφανον ἔχων χρυσοῦν καὶ διάδημα βύσσινον πορφυροῦν· ἰδόντες δὲ οἱ ἐν Σούσοις ἐχάρησαν. Τοῖς δὲ Ἰουδαίοις ἐγένετο φῶς καὶ εὐφροσύνη Κατὰ πόλιν καὶ χώραν οὗ ἂν ἐξετέθη τὸ πρόσταγμα, οὗ ἂν ἐξετέθη τὸ ἔκθεμα· χαρὰ καὶ εὐφροσύνη τοῖς Ἰουδαίοις, κώθων καὶ εὐφροσύνη· καὶ πολλοὶ τῶν ἐθνῶν περιετέμοντο καὶ Ἰου-δαΐζον διὰ τὸν φόβον τῶν Ἰουδαίων.

ἘΝ γὰρ τῷ δωδεκάτῳ μηνὶ τῇ τρισκαιδεκάτῃ

the month of Adar, on the
thirteenth day of the
same, when the order of
the king, and his decree,
was ready to be enforced,
that day those who oppos-
ed the Jews hoped to have
power over them although
it was not to be, for the
Jews were to rule over
those who hated them.

The Jews gathered all
of their people in their
cities throughout the
provinces of King Ahasuerus to take violence upon
those who would have hurt
them, and no person was
able to stop them for the
fear of the Jews fell upon
all of the people. All of
the rulers of the prov-
inces and their lieuten-
ants and the deputies and
officers of the king did
help the Jews because all
were afraid of Mordecai
[and what he would do to
them], for Mordecai was important in the king's
house, and his fame was
well known throughout the
empire; the man Mordecai
became increasingly more
important. For that rea-
son the Jews struck all of
their enemies with a
strike of the sword:
slaughtering and destroy-
ing, and doing that which

בִּשְׁלוֹשָׁה עָשָׂר יוֹם בּוֹ אֲשֶׁר הִגִּיעַ דְּבַר־
הַמֶּלֶךְ וְדָתוֹ לְהֵעָשׂוֹת בַּיּוֹם אֲשֶׁר שִׂבְּרוּ
אֹיְבֵי הַיְּהוּדִים לִשְׁלוֹט בָּהֶם וְנַהֲפוֹךְ הוּא
אֲשֶׁר יִשְׁלְטוּ הַיְּהוּדִים הֵמָּה בְּשֹׂנְאֵיהֶם :
נִקְהֲלוּ הַיְּהוּדִים בְּעָרֵיהֶם בְּכָל־מְדִינוֹת
הַמֶּלֶךְ אֲחַשְׁוֵרוֹשׁ לִשְׁלֹחַ יָד בִּמְבַקְשֵׁי
רָעָתָם וְאִישׁ לֹא־עָמַד בִּפְנֵיהֶם כִּי־נָפַל
פַּחְדָּם עַל־כָּל־הָעַמִּים : וְכָל־שָׂרֵי הַמְּדִינוֹת
וְהָאֲחַשְׁדַּרְפְּנִים וְהַפַּחוֹת וְעֹשֵׂי הַמְּלָאכָה
אֲשֶׁר לַמֶּלֶךְ מְנַשְּׂאִים אֶת־הַיְּהוּדִים כִּי־
נָפַל פַּחַד־מָרְדֳּכַי עֲלֵיהֶם : כִּי־גָדוֹל
מָרְדֳּכַי בְּבֵית הַמֶּלֶךְ וְשָׁמְעוֹ הוֹלֵךְ בְּכָל־
הַמְּדִינוֹת כִּי־הָאִישׁ מָרְדֳּכַי הוֹלֵךְ וְגָדוֹל :
וַיַּכּוּ הַיְּהוּדִים בְּכָל־אֹיְבֵיהֶם מַכַּת־חֶרֶב
וְהֶרֶג וְאַבְדָן וַיַּעֲשׂוּ בְשֹׂנְאֵיהֶם כִּרְצוֹנָם :

τοῦ μηνός, ὅς ἐστιν Ἀδάρ, παρῆν τὰ γράμματα
τὰ γραφέντα ὑπὸ τοῦ βασιλέως. Ἐν αὐτῇ τῇ
ἡμέρᾳ ἀπώλοντο οἱ ἀντικείμενοι τοῖς Ἰουδαίοις·
οὐδεὶς γὰρ ἀντέστη, φοβούμενος αὐτούς. Οἱ
γὰρ ἄρχοντες τῶν σατραπῶν καὶ οἱ τύραννοι καὶ
οἱ βασιλικοὶ γραμματεῖς ἐτίμων τοὺς Ἰουδαίους·
ὁ γὰρ φόβος Μαρδοχαίου ἐνέκειτο αὐτοῖς.
Προσέπεσε γὰρ τὸ πρόσταγμα τοῦ βασιλέως ὀνομασθῆναι ἐν πάσῃ τῇ βασιλείᾳ.

they wished to those that hated them. Even in the palace Shushan the Jews slew and destroyed five hundred men, as they did at Parshanda, Dalphon, Aspatha, Poratha, [and also] Adalia, Aridatha, Parmashta, Arisai, Aridai, and Vajezatha; and they slew the ten sons of Haman (who was the enemy of the Jews as a people), but they did not take spoils. On that day the number of those which were slain in Shushan palace were brought before the king. Then the king said to Queen Esther, "The Jews have slain five hundred men in Shushan palace, as well as the ten sons of Haman; what they have done in the rest of the king's province? Now what would you ask for? It will be granted to you or if you have any [et quid vis ut fieri jubeam] other request it will be done.

Esther replied, "If it pleases the king, let the Jews who are in Shushan be granted the right to do the same tomorrow what the decree allowed them to do today, and let Haman's ten sons be hanged from the gallows."

וּבְשׁוּשַׁן הַבִּירָה הָרְגוּ הַיְּהוּדִים וְאַבֵּד חֲמֵשׁ מֵאוֹת אִישׁ : וְאֵת ׀ פַּרְשַׁנְדָּתָא וְאֵת ׀ דַּלְפוֹן וְאֵת ׀ אַסְפָּתָא : וְאֵת ׀ פּוֹרָתָא וְאֵת ׀ אֲדַלְיָא וְאֵת ׀ אֲרִידָתָא : וְאֵת ׀ פַּרְמַשְׁתָּא וְאֵת ׀ אֲרִיסַי וְאֵת ׀ אֲרִידַי וְאֵת ׀ וַיְזָתָא : עֲשֶׂרֶת בְּנֵי הָמָן בֶּן־הַמְּדָתָא צֹרֵר הַיְּהוּדִים הָרָגוּ וּבַבִּזָּה לֹא שָׁלְחוּ אֶת־יָדָם : בַּיּוֹם הַהוּא בָּא מִסְפַּר הַהֲרוּגִים בְּשׁוּשַׁן הַבִּירָה לִפְנֵי הַמֶּלֶךְ : וַיֹּאמֶר הַמֶּלֶךְ לְאֶסְתֵּר הַמַּלְכָּה בְּשׁוּשַׁן הַבִּירָה הָרְגוּ הַיְּהוּדִים וְאַבֵּד חֲמֵשׁ מֵאוֹת אִישׁ וְאֵת עֲשֶׂרֶת בְּנֵי־הָמָן בִּשְׁאָר מְדִינוֹת הַמֶּלֶךְ מֶה עָשׂוּ וּמַה־שְּׁאֵלָתֵךְ וְיִנָּתֵן לָךְ וּמַה־בַּקָּשָׁתֵךְ עוֹד וְתֵעָשׂ : וַתֹּאמֶר אֶסְתֵּר

6 Καὶ ἐν Σούσοις τῇ πόλει ἀπέκτειναν οἱ Ἰουδαῖοι ἄνδρας πεντακοσίους, Τόν τε Φαρσαννὲς καὶ Δελφῶν καὶ Φασγὰ Καὶ Φαραδαθὰ καὶ Βαρεὰ καὶ Σαρβακὰ Καὶ Μαρμασιμὰ καὶ Ῥουφαῖον καὶ Ἀρταῖον καὶ Ζαβουθαῖον, Τοὺς δέκα υἱοὺς Ἀμὰν Ἀμαδάθου Βουγαίου τοῦ ἐχθροῦ τῶν Ἰουδαίων, καὶ διήρπασαν

Ἐν αὐτῇ τῇ ἡμέρᾳ· ἐπεδόθη τε ὁ ἀριθμὸς τῷ βασιλεῖ τῶν ἀπολωλότων ἐν Σούσοις. Εἶπε δὲ ὁ βασιλεὺς πρὸς Ἐσθήρ Ἀπώλεσαν οἱ Ἰουδαῖοι ἐν Σούσοις τῇ πόλει ἄνδρας πεντακοσίους· ἐν δὲ τῇ περιχώρῳ πῶς οἴει ἐχρήσαντο; τί οὖν ἀξιοῖς ἔτι καὶ ἔσται σοι; Καὶ εἶπεν Ἐσθὴρ τῷ

The king granted her request, and it was carried out at Shushan, and they hanged Haman's ten sons from the gallows.

The Jews then gathered on the fourteenth day of the month of Adar, and murdered three hundred [trecc viri] men who were at Shushan, but they did not take what they had. But the other Jews which were in the king's provinces assembled together and , leagued to protect their lives, resting in peace from their enemies; they had slain seventy-five thousand of their enemies but they did not take any booty.

On the thirteenth day of the month of Adar, and on the fourteenth day of the same, they rested, making it a day of feasting and merry-making. And the Jews that were at Shushan also assembled together on the thirteenth day and on the fourteenth day and the fifteenth day they too took a holiday and feasted and made merry. So did the Jews of the villages that lived in unwalled towns, making the fourteenth day of the month of Adar a day for

אִם־עַל־הַמֶּלֶךְ טוֹב יִנָּתֵן גַּם־מָחָר לַיְּהוּדִים אֲשֶׁר בְּשׁוּשָׁן לַעֲשׂוֹת כְּדָת הַיּוֹם וְאֵת עֲשֶׂרֶת בְּנֵי־הָמָן יִתְלוּ עַל־הָעֵץ: וַיֹּאמֶר הַמֶּלֶךְ לְהֵעָשׂוֹת כֵּן וַתִּנָּתֵן דָּת בְּשׁוּשָׁן וְאֵת עֲשֶׂרֶת בְּנֵי־הָמָן תָּלוּ: וַיִּקָּהֲלוּ הַיְּהוּדִיִּים אֲשֶׁר־בְּשׁוּשָׁן גַּם בְּיוֹם אַרְבָּעָה עָשָׂר לְחֹדֶשׁ אֲדָר וַיַּהַרְגוּ בְשׁוּשָׁן שְׁלֹשׁ מֵאוֹת אִישׁ וּבַבִּזָּה לֹא שָׁלְחוּ אֶת־יָדָם: וּשְׁאָר הַיְּהוּדִים אֲשֶׁר בִּמְדִינוֹת הַמֶּלֶךְ נִקְהֲלוּ ׀ וְעָמֹד עַל־נַפְשָׁם וְנוֹחַ מֵאֹיְבֵיהֶם וְהָרוֹג בְּשֹׂנְאֵיהֶם• חֲמִשָּׁה וְשִׁבְעִים אֶלֶף וּבַבִּזָּה לֹא שָׁלְחוּ אֶת־יָדָם: בְּיוֹם־ שְׁלוֹשָׁה עָשָׂר לְחֹדֶשׁ אֲדָר וְנוֹחַ בְּאַרְבָּעָה עָשָׂר בּוֹ וְעָשֹׂה אֹתוֹ יוֹם מִשְׁתֶּה וְשִׂמְחָה: וְהַיְּהוּדִיִּים אֲשֶׁר־בְּשׁוּשָׁן נִקְהֲלוּ בִּשְׁלוֹשָׁה עָשָׂר בּוֹ וּבְאַרְבָּעָה עָשָׂר בּוֹ וְנוֹחַ בַּחֲמִשָּׁה עָשָׂר בּוֹ וְעָשֹׂה אֹתוֹ יוֹם מִשְׁתֶּה וְשִׂמְחָה: עַל־כֵּן הַיְּהוּדִים הַפְּרָזִים הַיֹּשְׁבִים בְּעָרֵי הַפְּרָזוֹת עֹשִׂים אֵת יוֹם אַרְבָּעָה עָשָׂר לְחֹדֶשׁ אֲדָר שִׂמְחָה וּמִשְׁתֶּה וְיוֹם

βασιλεῖ Δοθήτω τοῖς Ἰουδαίοις χρῆσθαι ὡσαύτως τὴν αὔριον, ὥστε τοὺς δέκα υἱοὺς Ἀμὰν κρεμάσαι.

Καὶ ἐπέτρεψεν οὕτως γενέσθαι, καὶ ἐξέθηκε τοῖς Ἰουδαίοις τῆς πόλεως τὰ σώματα τῶν υἱῶν Ἀμὰν κρεμάσαι. Καὶ συνήχθησαν οἱ Ἰουδαῖοι ἐν Σούσοις τῇ τεσσαρεσκαιδεκάτῃ τοῦ Ἀδὰρ καὶ ἀπέκτειναν ἄνδρας τριακοσίους, καὶ οὐδὲν διήρπασαν. Οἱ δὲ λοιποὶ τῶν Ἰουδαίων οἱ ἐν τῇ βασιλείᾳ συνήχθησαν καὶ ἑαυτοῖς ἐβοήθουν, καὶ ἀνεπαύσαντο ἀπὸ τῶν πολεμίων · ἀπώλεσαν γὰρ αὐτῶν μυρίους πεντακισχιλίους τῇ τρισκαιδεκάτῃ τοῦ Ἀδάρ, καὶ οὐδὲν διήρπασαν. Καὶ ἀνεπαύ- σαντο τῇ τεσσαρεσκαιδεκάτῃ τοῦ αὐτοῦ μηνός, καὶ ἦγον αὐτὴν ἡμέραν ἀναπαύσεως μετὰ χαρᾶς

celebration and feasting.
I was a good day
and they sent presents to
one. Mordecai wrote
down these happenings,
sending letters to Jews
that lived in all of the
provinces of King
Ahasuerus, both those who
were close by, and those
who were at a great
distance, in order to
establish a tradition
among them that they were
to keep the fourteenth day
of the month of Adar, and
the fifteenth month of the
same [for a holiday] each
year, as a day when the
Jews knew peace from the
enemies they had. It was
a month which was turned
from sorrow to joy, and a
time to send presents to
one another, and [to send
freely] gifts to the poor
[Jews]. The Jews continu-
ed this celebration as Mordecai instructed, because
Haman, the son of [ilius Amadathi]
Hammedatha the Agagit,
the enemy of the Jews,
had plotted to destroy
all of them, having con-
cocted a plot to kill
them and bury them.
Esther went to the
king and he commanded
that the letters he had
sent to destroy the Jews

טוֹב וּמִשְׁלֹחַ מָנוֹת אִישׁ לְרֵעֵהוּ: וַיִּכְתֹּב
מָרְדֳּכַי אֶת־הַדְּבָרִים הָאֵלֶּה וַיִּשְׁלַח סְפָרִים
אֶל־כָּל־הַיְּהוּדִים אֲשֶׁר בְּכָל־מְדִינוֹת הַמֶּלֶךְ
אֲחַשְׁוֵרוֹשׁ הַקְּרוֹבִים וְהָרְחוֹקִים: לְקַיֵּם
עֲלֵיהֶם לִהְיוֹת עֹשִׂים אֵת יוֹם אַרְבָּעָה
עָשָׂר לְחֹדֶשׁ אֲדָר וְאֵת יוֹם־חֲמִשָּׁה עָשָׂר
בּוֹ בְּכָל־שָׁנָה וְשָׁנָה: כַּיָּמִים אֲשֶׁר־נָחוּ
בָהֶם הַיְּהוּדִים מֵאֹיְבֵיהֶם וְהַחֹדֶשׁ אֲשֶׁר
נֶהְפַּךְ לָהֶם מִיָּגוֹן לְשִׂמְחָה וּמֵאֵבֶל לְיוֹם
טוֹב לַעֲשׂוֹת אוֹתָם יְמֵי מִשְׁתֶּה וְשִׂמְחָה
וּמִשְׁלוֹחַ מָנוֹת אִישׁ לְרֵעֵהוּ וּמַתָּנוֹת
לָאֶבְיֹנִים: וְקִבֵּל הַיְּהוּדִים אֵת אֲשֶׁר־הֵחֵלּוּ
לַעֲשׂוֹת וְאֵת אֲשֶׁר־כָּתַב מָרְדֳּכַי אֲלֵיהֶם:
כִּי הָמָן בֶּן־הַמְּדָתָא הָאֲגָגִי צֹרֵר
כָּל־הַיְּהוּדִים חָשַׁב עַל־הַיְּהוּדִים לְאַבְּדָם
וְהִפִּיל פּוּר הוּא הַגּוֹרָל לְהֻמָּם וּלְאַבְּדָם:
וּבְבֹאָהּ לִפְנֵי הַמֶּלֶךְ אָמַר עִם־הַסֵּפֶר
יָשׁוּב מַחֲשַׁבְתּוֹ הָרָעָה אֲשֶׁר־חָשַׁב עַל־

καὶ εὐφροσύνης.   Οἱ δὲ Ἰουδαῖοι ἐν Σούσοις τῇ
πόλει συνήχθησαν καὶ τῇ τεσσαρεσκαιδεκάτῃ καὶ
ἀνεπαύσαντο· ἦγον δὲ καὶ τὴν πεντεκαιδεκάτην
μετὰ χαρᾶς καὶ εὐφροσύνης.   Διὰ τοῦτο οὖν
οἱ Ἰουδαῖοι οἱ διεσπαρμένοι ἐν πάσῃ χώρᾳ τῇ ἔξω
ἄγουσι τὴν τεσσαρεσκαιδεκάτην τοῦ Ἀδάρ ἡμέραν
ἀγαθὴν μετ᾽ εὐφροσύνης, ἀποστέλλοντες μερίδας
ἕκαστος τῷ πλησίον.   Ἔγραψε δὲ Μαρδοχαῖος
τοὺς λόγους τούτους εἰς βιβλίον, καὶ ἐξαπέστειλε
τοῖς Ἰουδαίοις ὅσοι ἦσαν ἐν τῇ Ἀρταξέρξου βασιλείᾳ τοῖς ἐγγὺς καὶ τοῖς μακράν,   Στῆσαι τὰς
ἡμέρας ταύτας ἀγαθάς, ἄγειν τε τὴν τεσσαρεσκαιδεκάτην καὶ τὴν πεντεκαιδεκάτην τοῦ Ἀδάρ·
Ἐν γὰρ ταύταις ταῖς ἡμέραις ἀνεπαύσαντο οἱ
Ἰουδαῖοι ἀπὸ τῶν ἐχθρῶν αὐτῶν· καὶ τὸν μῆνα
ἐν ᾧ ἐστράφη αὐτοῖς, ὃς ἦν Ἀδάρ, ἀπὸ πένθους

[because of Haman's plot]
be returned and their
instruction be placed on
[Haman and his sons] head
and life, so that he and
his sons [i.e. Haman and
his sons] should be hanged
from the gallows. For
this reason the Jews call
this set of days **Purim**,
after the name of Pur:
being the words of his
letter, and of that
which caused the pogrom
that they endured. The
Jews accepted this and vow-
ed to remember it and pass
its memory on to their
children, and upon all who
should convert to their
faith, so that the memory
of it would not be forgotten, and they would keep
it as a day of remembrance
by writing it down, and
celebrate it at the ap-
pointed time every year,
so that these days [of
tribulation] should be remembered and kept throughout every generation [and]
by every family, in every
province and in every
city, so that Purim will
not be forgotten by the
Jews, nor forgotten by any
of their future genera-
tions.

Queen Esther, daughter
of Abihail, and Mordecai

הַיְּהוּדִים עַל־רֹאשֵׁו וְתָלוּ אֹתוֹ וְאֶת־בָּנָיו
עַל־הָעֵץ : עַל־כֵּן קָרְאוּ לַיָּמִים הָאֵלֶּה
פּוּרִים עַל־שֵׁם הַפּוּר עַל־כֵּן עַל־כָּל־דִּבְרֵי
הָאִגֶּרֶת הַזֹּאת וּמָה־רָאוּ עַל־כָּכָה וּמָה
הִגִּיעַ אֲלֵיהֶם : קִיְּמוּ וְקִבְּלוּ הַיְּהוּדִים
עֲלֵיהֶם ׀ וְעַל־זַרְעָם וְעַל כָּל־הַנִּלְוִים
עֲלֵיהֶם וְלֹא יַעֲבוֹר לִהְיוֹת עֹשִׂים אֵת־שְׁנֵי
הַיָּמִים הָאֵלֶּה כִּכְתָבָם וְכִזְמַנָּם בְּכָל־שָׁנָה
וְשָׁנָה : וְהַיָּמִים הָאֵלֶּה נִזְכָּרִים וְנַעֲשִׂים
בְּכָל־דּוֹר וָדוֹר מִשְׁפָּחָה וּמִשְׁפָּחָה מְדִינָה
וּמְדִינָה וְעִיר וָעִיר וִימֵי הַפּוּרִים הָאֵלֶּה
לֹא יַעַבְרוּ מִתּוֹךְ הַיְּהוּדִים וְזִכְרָם לֹא־
יָסוּף מִזַּרְעָם : וַתִּכְתֹּב אֶסְתֵּר
הַמַּלְכָּה בַת־אֲבִיחַיִל וּמָרְדֳּכַי הַיְּהוּדִי
אֶת־כָּל־תֹּקֶף לְקַיֵּם אֵת אִגֶּרֶת הַפֻּרִים

εἰς χαρὰν καὶ ἀπὸ ὀδύνης εἰς ἀγαθὴν ἡμέραν,
ἄγειν ὅλον ἀγαθὰς ἡμέρας γάμων καὶ εὐφροσύνης, ἐξαποστέλλοντες μερίδας τοῖς φίλοις
καὶ τοῖς πτωχοῖς. Καὶ προσεδέξαντο οἱ
Ἰουδαῖοι καθὼς ἔγραψεν αὐτοῖς ὁ Μαρδοχαῖος,

Πῶς Ἀμὰν Ἀμαδάθου ὁ Μακεδὼν ἐπολέμει
αὐτούς, καθὼς ἔθετο ψήφισμα καὶ κλῆρον ἀφανίσαι
αὐτούς, Καὶ ὡς εἰσῆλθε πρὸς τὸν βασιλέα
λέγων κρεμάσαι τὸν Μαρδοχαῖον· ὅσα δὲ ἐπε-
χείρησεν ἐπάξαι ἐπὶ τοὺς Ἰουδαίους κακὰ ἐπ'
αὐτὸν ἐγένοντο, καὶ ἐκρεμάσθη αὐτὸς καὶ τὰ τέκνα
αὐτοῦ. Διὰ τοῦτο ἐπεκλήθησαν αἱ ἡμέραι αὗται
Φρουραὶ διὰ τοὺς κλήρους, ὅτι τῇ διαλέκτῳ αὐτῶν
καλοῦνται Φρουραί, διὰ τοὺς λόγους τῆς ἐπιστολῆς
ταύτης, καὶ ὅσα πεπόνθασι διὰ ταῦτα καὶ ὅσα
αὐτοῖς ἐγένετο, Καὶ ἔστησεν· καὶ προσεδέ-
χοντο οἱ Ἰουδαῖοι ἐφ' ἑαυτοῖς καὶ ἐπὶ τῷ σπέρματι
αὐτῶν καὶ ἐπὶ τοῖς προστεθειμένοις ἐπ' αὐτῶν,
οὐδὲ μὴν ἄλλως χρήσονται. Αἱ δὲ ἡμέραι αὗται
μνημόσυνον ἐπιτελούμενον κατὰ γενεὰν καὶ
γενεὰν καὶ πόλιν καὶ πατριὰν καὶ χώραν.

the Jew, wrote with authority all of these things,
confirming the second
letter of Purim.

And he [Mordecai]
sent the letters to all of
the Jews, to one hundred
and twenty-seven provinces
of the kingdom of Ahasuerus, containing words of
peace and truth. [The
king] did confirm the
times of Purim as Mordecai
and Queen Esther appointed
as they had ruled for themselves and for their fu-
ture generations, in the
matters of fasting and la-
mentations. The decree of
the Queen Esther confirm-
ing times as appointed Purim were written into his
book of chronicles.

He [the king] then
laid a tribute [tax] over
the land and on the
islands of the sea, and
all of the acts of his
reign, demonstrating is
might, declared the
greatness of Mordecai; and
the king advanced him, for
isn't it written in the
book of the chronicles
that is kept by the kings
of Media and Persia? For
Mordecai the Jew was next
to King Ahasueris, and a
great number of Jews were
also, and then increased

וַיִּשְׁלַח סְפָרִים אֶל־ : הַזֹּאת הַשֵּׁנִית
כָּל־הַיְּהוּדִים אֶל־שֶׁבַע וְעֶשְׂרִים וּמֵאָה
מְדִינָה מַלְכוּת אֲחַשְׁוֵרוֹשׁ דִּבְרֵי שָׁלוֹם
לְקַיֵּם אֶת־יְמֵי הַפֻּרִים הָאֵלֶּה : וֶאֱמֶת
בִּזְמַנֵּיהֶם כַּאֲשֶׁר קִיַּם עֲלֵיהֶם מָרְדֳּכַי
הַיְּהוּדִי וְאֶסְתֵּר הַמַּלְכָּה וְכַאֲשֶׁר קִיְּמוּ
עַל־נַפְשָׁם וְעַל־זַרְעָם דִּבְרֵי הַצֹּמוֹת
וּמַאֲמַר אֶסְתֵּר קִיַּם דִּבְרֵי : וְזַעֲקָתָם
הַפֻּרִים הָאֵלֶּה וְנִכְתָּב בַּסֵּפֶר :

וַיָּשֶׂם הַמֶּלֶךְ אֲחַשְׁרֵשׁ ׀ מַס עַל־הָאָרֶץ
וְכָל־מַעֲשֵׂה תָקְפּוֹ וּגְבוּרָתוֹ : וְאִיֵּי הַיָּם
וּפָרָשַׁת גְּדֻלַּת מָרְדֳּכַי אֲשֶׁר גִּדְּלוֹ הַמֶּלֶךְ
הֲלוֹא־הֵם כְּתוּבִים עַל־סֵפֶר דִּבְרֵי הַיָּמִים

Αἱ δὲ ἡμέραι αὗται τῶν Φρουραὶ ἀχθήσον-
ται εἰς τὸν ἅπαντα χρόνον, καὶ τὸ μνημόσυνον
αὐτῶν οὐ μὴ ἐκλίπῃ ἐκ τῶν γενεῶν.   Καὶ
ἔγραψεν Ἐσθὴρ ἡ βασίλισσα θυγάτηρ Ἀμιναδὰβ καὶ Μαρδοχαῖος ὁ Ἰουδαῖος ὅσα ἐποίησαν
τό τε στερέωμα τῆς ἐπιστολῆς τῶν Φρουραί.
    Καὶ Μαρδοχαῖος καὶ Ἐσθὴρ ἡ βασίλισσα
ἔστησαν ἑαυτοῖς καθ' ἑαυτῶν, καὶ τότε στήσαντες
κατὰ τῆς ὑγιείας ἑαυτῶν καὶ τὴν βουλὴν αὐτῶν.
    Καὶ Ἐσθὴρ λόγῳ ἔστησεν εἰς τὸν αἰῶνα, καὶ
ἐγράφη εἰς μνημόσυνον.
    ἜΓΡΑΨΕ δὲ ὁ βασιλεὺς ἐπὶ τὴν βασιλείαν
τῆς τε γῆς καὶ τῆς θαλάσσης ·   Καὶ τὴν ἰσχὺν
αὐτοῦ καὶ ἀνδραγαθίαν, πλοῦτόν τε καὶ δόξαν
τῆς βασιλείας αὐτοῦ, ἰδοὺ γέγραπται ἐν βιβλίῳ

the wealth of his people,
and spoke of peace of all
of his descendents.

לַמְּלָכֵי מָדַי וּפָרָס : כִּי ׀ מָרְדֳּכַי הַיְּהוּדִי
מִשְׁנֶה לַמֶּלֶךְ אֲחַשְׁוֵרוֹשׁ וְגָדוֹל לַיְּהוּדִים
וְרָצוּי לְרֹב אֶחָיו דֹּרֵשׁ טוֹב לְעַמּוֹ וְדֹבֵר
שָׁלוֹם לְכָל־זַרְעוֹ :

βασιλέων Περσῶν καὶ Μήδων εἰς μνημόσυνον.
Ὁ δὲ Μαρδοχαῖος διεδέχετο τὸν βασιλέα Ἀρταξέρξην, καὶ μέγας ἦν ἐν τῇ βασιλείᾳ καὶ δεδοξα-
σμένος ὑπὸ τῶν Ἰουδαίων · καὶ φιλούμενος διηγεῖτο
τὴν ἀγωγὴν παντὶ τῷ ἔθνει αὐτοῦ.

The story of Esther presents a uniquely can-
did picture of the life of women in Babylon. They
were maintained in a harem where the sole occupa-
tion or purpose was to sexually satisfy the man.
If there was more than one wife in the harem each
woman might only have a single opportunity in a
life time to be with her husband. And then that
particular opportunity or time would come only
when he had called her because of his own physical
needs, which were frequently stirred by drinking
too much wine. It is apparent that celebrations
centered around wine consumption; in fact the majority of the celebrations were devoted exclusive-
ly to wine consumption.

If a woman attempted to exert herself and
demonstrate some autonomy, she could be divorced
if she were the wife of the king. Very young
girls were especially popular replacements, and
again their purpose was sexual. However, if the
replacement was beautiful and young she could in
many cases covertly control the ruler, as was the
case of Esther.

The account of Esther brings forward the
extreme barbarity of the age, the constant quest

for rising socially and economically regardless of cost, and the cheapness with which life was regarded. Hatred for the Jews was as common then as it was in the days of Nazi Germany. The Jews did suffer, but when they had an opportunity to better their circumstances they concentrated on revenge, a very human desire. Esther does temper this situation after the majority of the vengance had run its course, but limiting the days, and then satisfying the need to remember it by declaring the days that it transmorgified from a common unity into a massacre to be a holiday.

Later generations of Jews that lived in Babylon did not do as well. The discrimination continued as increasing numbers of Babylonians saw the Jews as socially deviant: not speaking the same language, worshipping the same gods, holding the same customs, or recognizing the same past. Because there was no assimilation of the Jews into the Babylonian culture because the Jews were determined to remain a separate people, persecutions and discriminations increased and intensified. So sharp was the line drawn between the two civilizations that when Babylon was beseiged the Jews celebrated its promised destruction, eventhough the destruction of Babylon might have led to their own-- so intense was their hatred for Babylon.

Babylon fell, first to the Medes, and then to the Persians. Their women who had experienced a minor advance, were thrown backwards into the discriminatory practices and prohibitions of the past, until Xerxes came to power. His ascent saw a rejuvination of equality, and he personally recognized and employed women as equals to men.

Persia

Sweeping westward across Babylon, the Persians appeared unbeatable as they marched as conquerors into Egypt. Women were especially important to the Persian rulers, not so much out of sexual needs or desires, but because men were scarce. Since men were scarce the leaders of Persian society, including the kings of Persia, turned to women to fill the void.

Women participated in every field and on every plateau in Persian history, including the military. They were astute businesspersons, shopkeepers, currency exchangers, and police. Even the traditional balliwick of men, the military, boasted of women who filled the ranks from private to admiral. Xerxes was especially prone to use women in his quest to control Greece in 480 B. C.

The admiral most feared by the Greeks was the woman Artemisia, whose successes Herodotus painfully recorded:

I name none of the rest of the capitans, there being no need to do so, except for Artemisia who moves me to marvel greatly that a woman should have gone with armament against the Hellas; for her husband being dead, she herself having had his sovereignity and a young son too, followed the host without any want for necessities, but she was strong hearted and valorous.

Artemisia was her name. She was the daughter to Lygdamis, of Halicarnassian lineage on her father's side, and on her mother's she was a Cretan. She was the leader of the men of Halicarnassus and Cos and Nisyrus and Calydnos, furnishing five ships. Her ships were reputed the best in the entire fleet after the ships of Sidon; and, of all of his allies, she gave the king the best counsels. The cities, of where I said she was the leader, are all of Dorian stock, as I can show, the Hallicarnassians being of Troezen and the rest of Epidaurus. [29]

Τῶν μέν νυν ἄλλων οὐ παραμέμνημαι
ταξιάρχων ὡς οὐκ ἀναγκαζόμενος, Ἀρτεμισίης
δὲ τῆς μάλιστα θῶμα ποιεῦμαι ἐπὶ τὴν Ἑλλάδα
στρατευσαμένης γυναικός· ἥτις ἀποθανόντος τοῦ
ἀνδρὸς αὐτή τε ἔχουσα τὴν τυραννίδα καὶ παιδὸς
ὑπάρχοντος νεηνίεω ὑπὸ λήματός τε καὶ ἀνδρηίης
ἐστρατεύετο, οὐδεμιῆς οἱ ἐούσης ἀναγκαίης. οὔνομα
μὲν δὴ ἦν αὐτῇ Ἀρτεμισίη, θυγάτηρ δὲ ἦν Λυγδά-
μιος, γένος δὲ ἐξ Ἁλικαρνησσοῦ τὰ πρὸς πατρός,
τὰ μητρόθεν δὲ Κρῆσσα. ἡγεμόνευε δὲ Ἁλι-
καρνησσέων τε καὶ Κώων καὶ Νισυρίων τε καὶ
Καλυδνίων, πέντε νέας παρεχομένη. καὶ συνα-
πάσης τῆς στρατιῆς, μετά γε τὰς Σιδωνίης, νέας
εὐδοξοτάτας παρείχετο πάντων τε τῶν συμμάχων

γνώμας ἀρίστας βασιλέι ἀπεδέξατο. τῶν δὲ
κατέλεξα πολίων ἡγεμονεύειν αὐτήν, τὸ ἔθνος
ἀποφαίνω πᾶν ἐὸν Δωρικόν, Ἁλικαρνησσέας μὲν
Τροιζηνίους, τοὺς δὲ ἄλλους Ἐπιδαυρίους.

Artemisia was no token admiral. Universally feared, Herodotus even shows some coy respect, as he continued:

In that sea fight the nations that won most renown were the Aeginetans, and next to them the Athenians. Among men the most renowned were Polycritus of Aegina and two Athenians: Eumenes of Anagyrus and Aminias of Pallene, he who pursued after

66

Artemisia. Had he known that she was in that ship he had never been stayed from either taking her ship or losing his own--such was the binding given to the Athenian captain, and there was a prize of no less than ten thousand drachmae for whoever should take her alive: for there was universal anger that a woman should come to attack Athens. But she escaped as I already have said; and the rest of the ships too were not destroyed at Phalerum.[30]

Ἐν δὲ τῇ ναυμαχίῃ ταύτῃ ἤκουσαν Ἑλ-
λήνων ἄριστα Αἰγινῆται, ἐπὶ δὲ Ἀθηναῖοι,
ἀνδρῶν δὲ Πολύκριτός τε ὁ Αἰγινήτης καὶ
Ἀθηναῖοι Εὐμένης τε ὁ Ἀναγυράσιος καὶ Ἀμεινίης
Παλληνεύς, ὃς καὶ Ἀρτεμισίην ἐπεδίωξε. εἰ μέν
νυν ἔμαθε ὅτι ἐν ταύτῃ πλέοι Ἀρτεμισίη, οὐκ
ἂν ἐπαύσατο πρότερον ἢ εἷλέ μιν ἢ καὶ αὐτὸς
ἥλω. τοῖσι γὰρ Ἀθηναίων τριηράρχοισι παρε-
κεκέλευστο, πρὸς δὲ καὶ ἄεθλον ἔκειτο μύριαι
δραχμαί, ὃς ἄν μιν ζωὴν ἕλῃ· δεινὸν γάρ τι
ἐποιεῦντο γυναῖκα ἐπὶ τὰς Ἀθήνας στρατεύεσθαι.
αὕτη μὲν δή, ὡς πρότερον εἴρηται, διέφυγε· ἦσαν
δὲ καὶ οἱ ἄλλοι, τῶν αἱ νέες περιεγεγόνεσαν, ἐν
τῷ Φαλήρῳ.

Artemisia was a first-rate strategist, and patriot. She was also an able thinker whose advise was better than most men, as seen in her consultation with Mardonius:

"..if you make hast to fight at once on the sea, I fear that your fleet will come to harm and thereby your army will also come to hurt. Moreover, O King, remember this: good men's slaves are seldom evil, and bad men's slaves are seldom good; and you, who are the best of all men have evil slaves who pass as your allies: men of Egypt, and Cyprus, and Cilicia, and Pamphylia, in whom there is no usefulness.

"When Artemisia spoke in this manner to Mardonius, all that were her friends were sorry for her words, thinking that the king would do her some hurt for counselling him against a sea-fight; but they that had worries and were jealous over her because of the honor in which she was held above all the allies were pleased with her answer thinking that it would be her undoing. But when the opinons were reported to Xerxes he was greatly pleased by the opinion of Artemisia: he had for a long time deemed her a woman of worth and now held her in much higher esteem. Nevertheless, he accepted the counsel of the majority and ordered it to be followed, for he believed that off [the coast of] Euobea his men had been slack fighters by reason of his absence, and now he purposed to watch the battle himself." [31]

Ἐπεὶ δὲ περιιὼν εἰρώτα ὁ Μαρδόνιος ἀρξά-
μενος ἀπὸ τοῦ Σιδωνίου, οἱ μὲν ἄλλοι κατὰ
τώυτὸ γνώμην ἐξεφέροντο κελεύοντες ναυμαχίην
ποιέεσθαι, Ἀρτεμισίη δὲ τάδε ἔφη. " Εἰπεῖν μοι
πρὸς βασιλέα, Μαρδόνιε, ὡς ἐγὼ τάδε λέγω, οὔτε
κακίστη γενομένη ἐν τῇσι ναυμαχίῃσι τῇσι πρὸς
Εὐβοίῃ οὔτε ἐλάχιστα ἀποδεξαμένη. δέσποτα,
τὴν δὲ ἐοῦσαν γνώμην με δίκαιον ἐστὶ ἀποδεί-
κνυσθαι, τὰ τυγχάνω φρονέουσα ἄριστα ἐς πρήγματα τὰ σά. καί τοι τάδε λέγω, φείδεο τῶν νεῶν
μηδὲ ναυμαχίην ποιέο. οἱ γὰρ ἄνδρες τῶν σῶν
ἀνδρῶν κρέσσονες τοσοῦτο εἰσὶ κατὰ θάλασσαν
ὅσον ἄνδρες γυναικῶν. τί δὲ πάντως δέει σε
ναυμαχίῃσι ἀνακινδυνεύειν; οὐκ ἔχεις μὲν τὰς
Ἀθήνας, τῶν περ εἵνεκα ὁρμήθης στρατεύεσθαι,
ἔχεις δὲ τὴν ἄλλην Ἑλλάδα; ἐμποδὼν δέ τοι
ἵσταται οὐδείς· οἱ δέ τοι ἀντέστησαν, ἀπήλλαξαν
οὕτω ὡς κείνους ἔπρεπε. τῇ δὲ ἐγὼ δοκέω ἀπο-
βήσεσθαι τὰ τῶν ἀντιπολέμων πρήγματα, τοῦτο
φράσω. ἢν μὲν μὴ ἐπειχθῇς ναυμαχίην ποιεύ-
μενος, ἀλλὰ τὰς νέας αὐτοῦ ἔχῃς πρὸς γῇ μένων
ἢ καὶ προβαίνων ἐς τὴν Πελοπόννησον, εὐπετέως

τοι δέσποτα χωρήσει τὰ νοέων ἐλήλυθας. οὐ
γὰρ οἷοί τε πολλὸν χρόνον εἰσί τοι ἀντέχειν οἱ
Ἕλληνες, ἀλλὰ σφέας διασκεδᾷς, κατὰ πόλις δὲ
ἕκαστοι φεύξονται. οὔτε γὰρ σῖτος πάρα σφι ἐν
τῇ νήσῳ ταύτῃ, ὡς ἐγὼ πυνθάνομαι, οὔτε αὐτοὺς
οἰκός, ἢν σὺ ἐπὶ τὴν Πελοπόννησον ἐλαύνῃς τὸν
πεζὸν στρατόν, ἀτρεμιεῖν τοὺς ἐκεῖθεν αὐτῶν
ἥκοντας, οὐδέ σφι μελήσει πρὸ. τῶν Ἀθηνέων
ναυμαχέειν. ἢν δὲ αὐτίκα ἐπειχθῇς ναυμαχῆσαι,
δειμαίνω μὴ ὁ ναυτικὸς στρατὸς κακωθεὶς τὸν
πεζὸν προσδηλήσηται. πρὸς δὲ, ὦ βασιλεῦ, καὶ
τόδε ἐς θυμὸν βάλευ, ὡς τοῖσι μὲν χρηστοῖσι
τῶν ἀνθρώπων κακοὶ δοῦλοι φιλέουσι γίνεσθαι,
τοῖσι δὲ κακοῖσι χρηστοί. σοὶ δὲ ἐόντι ἀρίστῳ
ἀνδρῶν πάντων κακοὶ δοῦλοι εἰσί, οἳ ἐν συμμάχων
λόγῳ λέγονται εἶναι ἐόντες Αἰγύπτιοί τε καὶ
Κύπριοι καὶ Κίλικες καὶ Πάμφυλοι, τῶν ὄφελος
ἐστὶ οὐδέν."

Ταῦτα λεγούσης πρὸς Μαρδόνιον, ὅσοι μὲν
ἦσαν εὔνοοι τῇ Ἀρτεμισίῃ, συμφορὴν ἐποιεῦντο
τοὺς λόγους ὡς κακόν τι πεισομένης πρὸς βασι-
λέος, ὅτι οὐκ ἔα ναυμαχίην ποιέεσθαι· οἳ δὲ
ἀγεόμενοί τε καὶ φθονέοντες αὐτῇ, ἅτε ἐν πρώτοισι
τετιμημένης διὰ πάντων τῶν συμμάχων, ἐτέρποντο
τῇ ἀνακρίσι ὡς ἀπολεομένης αὐτῆς. ἐπεὶ δὲ
ἀνηνείχθησαν αἱ γνῶμαι ἐς Ξέρξην, κάρτα τε
ἥσθη τῇ γνώμῃ τῇ Ἀρτεμισίης, καὶ νομίζων ἔτι
πρότερον σπουδαίην εἶναι τότε πολλῷ μᾶλλον
αἴνεε. ὅμως δὲ τοῖσι πλέοσι πείθεσθαι ἐκέλευε,
τάδε καταδόξας, πρὸς μὲν Εὐβοίῃ σφέας ἐθελο-
κακέειν ὡς οὐ παρεόντος αὐτοῦ, τότε δὲ αὐτὸς
παρεσκεύαστο θεήσασθαι ναυμαχέοντας.

One can speculate on what the possible out-
come might have been if the counsel of Artemisia
had been followed. Xerxes lost. And by losing
Xerxes (or, in Persian **Khshayarsha**), returned
home, taking with some booty, but little Greek culture: the women therefore remained slightly more
free than the women trapped in the **gynaceum,** and
enjoyed the basic civil liberties as recorded in

the Code of Hamurabi. Yet these women, like most other women in the ancient Near East were not as free as the women of Egypt.

Tomb of Djeserkareseneb, Thebes
The daughters of a high bureaucrat are presenting him with a decorative neckband and a bowl of liquor. Hirmer Fotoarchiv

(Below) Queen Hatshepsut
After seizing power, Hatshepsut took the title of king and had herself portrayed in the traditional pose and costume of a male ruler. The Metropolitan Museum of Art, Rogers Fund and contributions from Edward S. Harkness, 1929

Egypt

The world of ancient Egypt was unlike any other known world in the records of time. The Greek historian, Herodotus, in the fifth century called Egypt "the gift of the Nile." And it was this single geographic factor, the might Nile river, that fashioned the history and destiny of Egypt, as well as it religion, philosophy, economics and life style.

Compared to other waters, the Nile was gentle to its people. It fertilized and renewed the land each September when it flooded the valley, transforming it into an uniquely rich alluvian marsh. When its waters receeded in November the Nile valley boasted a think covering of nutrient rich, fertile mude ready to be planted with crops.[32]

The men and women who lived o n the land were, for the most part, common people. They stood at the bottom of the social and economic level of society, and were always at the mercy of a venial and corrupt officialdom which was personified in the person of the hated, grasping tax collector.

It was not uncommon for the citizen to be beaten, bound, and even thrown into a well ("soused and dipped head downwards" with "his wife...bound in his presence and his children in fetters" if he was slow in remitting twenty percent of his harvest in taxes.[33]

Fortunately Egypt's legal system did permit civil complaints, and sometimes civil citizen litigation was decided in the favor of the plantiff: peasant or laborer. However, seldom was a slave able to bring a case to court; there is no record of a slave every winning a judgement. But slavery was not a part of the Egyptian society until the New Kingdom (cr. 1570-1075 B.C.).

Egypt was unique inasmuch as it had neither a caste, nor a class system that was rigidly entrenched. Private ingenuity could gain unlimited rewards. A slave could become a chief administrator (as in the case of the Hebrew Joseph) if s/he acquired and perfected a rare or special talent. Eventhough this social mobility was available to all, most Egyptians remained tied to the land out of a piety unmatched elsewhere. The majority of the Egyptians saw the land as their original mother: to leave the land was tantamount to severing the family ties. Others were subjected to toiling the land because they had either become endebted and thus were sold as slaves to pay off their debts, or were foreign slaves brought in after war. Those which worked on the land but did not till the soil were those who worked on pyrimids and canals either out of a special belief in their actions (seeing their labor as a devotion to the god-king/queen), or because they had been drafted by the pharaoh who wished to see his/her final resting place perfected prior to leaving the life enjoyed on earth. There was little complaint about this labor.initially, for the majority of those who worked believed that to defy the will of pharaoh would bring to Egypt and their home plagues, pestilences, and problems that had not yet been experienced.

Women played an especially important role in Egypt, for Egypt was strictly matriarchal and matrilineal in nature. Their contributions were in every area, from irrigation innovations to empire expansion .

The records of the contributions of women to Egyptian civilization and history are more plentiful after North Egypt joined South Egypt, fashioning its capital at the biblical city of On, which the Egyptians dedicated to the sun-god calling it Heliopolis.   This   initial   union   however

was not to endure long, for the south became tired
of supporting the impoverished of the north and declared its independence. Civil war raged, and unlike American history the south won. Their victory however did not lead to a separation between
the two Egypts; on the contrary it was opposite,
for once that the south had won she pulled the two
Egypts closer together but under her own economic,
social, and political philosophy. The individual
who led in this coup was named Menes.

With few exceptions the history of ancient
Egypt is written as a closed, xenophobic and xeno-
centric history. The Egyptians seldom left their
land, and if they did it was for commercial activity or war; even then their exodus was temporary,
and soon those who had left returned to the valley
of the Nile, praising the deities for their safe
return.

From their formative years on, Egypt not
only did not welcome innovations, but made valiant
efforts to keep new ideas and ways of doing pro-
jects out of the Nile valley. Fortunate for the
Egyptians this did not lead to a socio-regression.
On the contrary, Egypt continued to grow and ex-
pand in every way, making her people one of the
most refined in the civilized world, and giving to
them one of the most advanced cultures. All of
the arts and the sciences flourished, for the
Egyptians were generally not an aggressive people;
instead, they had time to relax and proceed un-
hurriedly towards stable and advancing visccisi-
tudes and heights, as witnessed by the frescoes
and bas-reliefs depicting their joy of living,
humor, and prosperity. As is acknowledged by most
Aegyptologists, "for the ordinary Egyptian, the
good moments of life
outnumbered the bad."

Egypt

Early Egyptian existence was little more than that. Life centered around food gathering. This, in time, was supplemented with food hunting, and meats appeared in the diet. Men and women equally participated in the quest for foods. They used knives, arrows, and rudimentary spears when hunting, and when they began to break the soil and cultivate grains they invented hoes and a primitive plow.

From the earliest records we find that this industrious people produced a surplus. Raising more grain than they could consume at one time, the Egyptians invented the silo to store their grains. These silos were made as waterproof as was possible then, and their floors were lined with mats so that the grain would not come in contact with the earth.

Marketing suprlus goods brought the early Egyptians new materials and prosperity. This increased standard of living made life more leisurely. Now there was time for sewing, weaving, cooking, baking, and the manufacture of fine combs, beads, and bracelets. At the same time a full range of cosmetics and perfumes were invented which delighted both the Egyptian men and women, for cosmetics and ungents were applied lavishly by both sexes. Of these cosmetics the most luxurious and costly was an eye paint made from genuine green malachite, which was considered not only special but equally sacred.

By 3000 B.C., Egypt gave up the nomadic life. Now Egyptian builders designed and perfected a general purpose mud brick which had the distinction of being the first building material to be produced of a standard size. Additionally these early masons produced smaller, more decorative bricks which were reinforced with either sand or straw.

Although the Egyptians had kilns to bake their bricks, for some, yet unexplained reason, they preferred sun-dried bricks. A possible explanation could be centered around their intense devotion to the sun, and belief that anything firmed by the sun had the deity's special blessing.

Regardless of the brick created, most were used locally. (The remaining bricks were later marketed abroad which increased the Egyptian treasury.) To add strength to the basic larger brick, linen strips were added for reinforcement, and soon the construction industry boomed, so that within several generations the majority of the citizenry enjoyed the protection of real brick dwellings against the intense sun, heat, and wind.

The materials which fashioned the walls of the early Egyptian homes was the same material as used for the floors and ceilings (and roofs). The floors were, with few exceptions, made out of a mud plaster over which gypsum was installed.

By studying the **mastaba** tombs (or "houses of the dead") we can better understand the "houses of the living." In nearly every case the houses of the living was composed of several rooms. Rooms for the storage of grains, cattle, and other livestock were the same as the residential room(s) which were all in the same building. The more affluent enjoyed the special advantage of having homes composed of several floors; in such cases the living quarters of the homeowner were separated from the storage rooms, and the quarters for livestock and servants. The former rooms were usually on the second or higher floors, while the latter was on the ground floor.

The exceptionally affluent were able to afford fine villas. These were located either in the countryside, or in the prosperous upper class superbs of Memphis or Thebes. In each case they were away from the cramped and overcrowded conditions endured by the very poor which made up the bulk of ancient Egyptian civilization.

To further segregate themselves from the destitute, the wealthy few built tall, elaborately

scalloped toppedf walls around their villas.
There was only one entrance into their compounds:
through stout double doors set in a gateway shpaed
like a miniature pylon.

In order to soften the interior of the Egyptian home, climbing plants trained to intertwine,
latticed timbers which fronted square pools of
water on which pink waterlilies. Around these
pools were planted lavish gardens of flowers and
vegetables which were shaded by palm trees.

Early Egyptian homes were fashioned with
stark straight lines. There were no windows: only
grilles set up high in the walls. Such homes usually boasted twenty-four to thirty rooms, however, although seldom were all of the rooms used.

Entrance into these larger homes was by way
of a long hall in which visitors and guests gathered after they had passed through the front gate
which was protected with a pet dog. The entrance
hall was embellished with a double row of columns
which were made out of wood and placed on stone
bases. Their capitals were imitations of papyrus
leaves, and frequently were painted to resemble
nature.

The entrance hall led into a main receiving
room. This court room had loft ceilings, and was
approximately thirty feet square, serving as both
a drawing room and a dining room after the general
pleasantries had been exchanged.

On a raised hearth a small brazier gave
needed heat in the winter. Around it were rugs
and cushions for the host family and their guests
to recline on while eating or conversing. Near
the couches were stationary water jugs of
beautifully painted pottery. From these jugs
water (or wine) was drawn throughout the eating
period; those jugs which held water were dipped into to wash the dust and sand picked up outdoors
and carried into the house. The jugs which held
wine were then tipped to pour their contents into
smartly shaped pitchers which servants carried

around to the guests' outstretched goblets.

From the couches the guests could not only see and talk with one another, but they could see into the adjoining rooms. The most important room off of the central great hall was the family shrine. If the family was of moderate means this shrine would be small (the low income families kept their shrine in a cupboard, while the destitute, if they had a shrine at all, mounted it on a small shelf), while the wealthy sometimes had rooms larger than their own bedrooms to welcome and house the deities.

Other rooms off of the central room were more private chambers: especially the bedrooms. Bathrooms, too, existed, but only for the very well-to-do. The bathrooms of the well-to-do were quite modern by current twentieth century standards. They boasted pipes and other plumbings. The lavoratory seat (modern by any standard), wash basins, and the like were strong enough to support the weight of the most ample, as well as generous enough in design to permit total usage.

The wealthy also enjoyed a brisk massage. It was given while they lay on a marble slab. Not only was their skin massaged, but their body completely bathed and cared for by servants (and an occasional professional masseur). The massage was not the reality only for the men, but was equally enjoyed by the women as well.

Women in ancient Egypt had a unique position in the social world of the major cities. Not only were they considered equal to men, but they were treated on par with men.

There was little difference in the hair-styles of Egyptian men and women. Both of the sexes wore it long, frequently braiding it or knotting it if they lived in cool climates, bor shaving it completely off in warmer areas of the dual-kingdom. On special occasions they donned elaborately curled wigs which were combed and pomaded. This was always a marked contrast to the traditionally unkept foreigner.

Sometimes Egyptian women went further than Egyptian men in completing their toilette. This was especially true on special occasions.

Preparations for holidays and festivals in ancient Egypt saw Egyptian women elaborately styl-ing their hair (or wigs) by embellishing it with bands of beads or metals, tasselled ribbons, or tiaras. Frequently it was fixed with wax and then richly perfumed. The wax most of the time melted at social gatherings, but instead of experiencing embarrassment, discomfort, and/or frustration, both the men and the women enjoyed the experience, for the melted wax laved the wearer with a sweet scent, adding a new vitality to a rather suffocat-ing experience.

In the country men and women alike wore little clothing, and then it was because they were receiving little known or seldom visited guests. Most of the time both men and women passed through life in the garmets nature had given them at the moment of their birth. The Egyptian attitude to-wards nudity to any degree was totally unselfcon-scious, which tended to shock more puritanic civil-izations.

When clothing was worn it was at best a simple, basic piece of linen. Men wore it over the loincloth, while women draped it over their petticoat or shift. Only during ceremonies was there a noticable difference between the rich and the poor. During such times the rich would put on a robe made from the finest linen to which would be affixed a shoulder strap if it was not worn loosely, and then tied at the waist with a wide stripe of linen which was knotted in such a way as to give the appearance of being a triangular apron. In this regard only women occasionally deviated: wearing, instead, a sari-like robe which was enhanced by a colorful array of necklaces and bracelets.

Rich or poor, male or female, the love of jewelry was universal in ancient Egyptian society. It layered necks, wrists, ankles, feet, even hands and loins. Jewelry was not worn only for the aesthetics, but also as charms for their magical powress to prevent sicknesses and ward off evil.

The most common piece of jewelry was the elaborate beaded collar. It was worn since the very earliest days, and consisted of rows of tubular beads divided by circular beads. Generally this collar was three inches wide, but occasionally it was broader, covering the entire upper shoulders of the wearer; this luxury, however, was only enjoyed by the ennobled or the very rich.

Women preferred green malachite as their main jewel. There exists many records (hieroglyphics and parchment inscriptions) which detail the women's love for adornments, and the elaborate and painstaking toilet they went through in preparation to wear her marks of man-created beauty. After a thorough washing of her body (a phenomena approach a fetish, for all Egyptians would would be clean at all costs, were) she shampooed her hair with salts and a paste added amply to water to friz her hair into an elaborate hair-do. Hairstyling then became her great passion. The higher it was piled or the more intricate the knotting was, the more the women were satisfied.

Once the Egyptian woman's hair was settled into a suitablely stylish coiffeur, she began working on her face. This process was even more time consuming, and was probably her most ambitious labor for the day since it took nearly the entire day to complete. She used salves and unguents, a little palette for mixing cosmetics and eyepaints, employing a pumice stone for removing superfluous hair and even for the trimming and shaping of her eyebrow. If any part displeased her she started all over again.

The most critical and important part of the woman's appearance were her eyes. The eyes mirrored the soul, all Egyptians believed, and since this was the case both men and women toiled tediously for hours to make their eye cosmetics reflect their best. With black ink and other pigments she (as did man) fashioned an eye line to represent an almond. She would draw thick rings around each eye and then darken the lids in many layers of malachite.

Red ochre would be used in dramatizing her lips and cheeks. The brillance of the color for the sake of the color was more important than the successful employment to bring out her best natural self, so suttle shading was not sought since such pale color adornment was a mark of poverty.

Egyptian woman also tinted her nails. Henna was the most popular color, and she used a little henna to redden her palms and even the soles of her feet.

Finally, as the toilette drew to a close, she would sent her entire body with oils and perfumes. A final touch of scarlet to the inside of her nails was the completing act. (As the empire grew in size and wealth, so too did her toilette.)

Adorned and perfumed Egyptian woman were openly welcomed into the company of men.* With few

---

*Cp.: Οἱ ἱρέες τῶν θεῶν τῇ μὲν ἄλλῃ κομέουσι, ἐν Αἰγύπτῳ δὲ ξυρῶνται. τοῖσι ἄλλοισι ἀνθρώποισι νόμος ἅμα κήδεϊ κεκάρθαι τὰς κεφαλὰς τοὺς μάλιστα ἱκνέεται, Αἰγύπτιοι δὲ ὑπὸ τοὺς θανάτους ἀνιεῖσι τὰς τρίχας αὔξεσθαι τάς τε ἐν τῇ κεφαλῇ καὶ τῷ γενείῳ, τέως ἐξυρημένοι.

exceptions, however, women entered the company of men only with their husbands. They were totally comfortable in such situations, unlike their foreign sisters. They sat beside their husbands in a relaxed atmosphere; frequently the husband put his arms around his wife's shoulders, but the majority of the time they visited with their friends with the husband's hand placed close and lovingly over the wife's. Except for the ancient Etruscans, few other contemporary societies enjoyed such an open familiarity and affection.

Younger women were also at such gatherings, but then moreso as entertainers than as visitors. During these times, singing and dancing or playing on lyres, their beauty and skills were appraised by father's seeking suitable mates for their sons.

Marriage was a true partnership in ancient Egypt. The woman was loved, held in respect, and consulted. She was an equal team member. She enjoyed special attention and respect since the first goddess of the Egyptian world was a woman who had traveled throughout Egypt and as far as Syria to retrieve the portions of her husband's dismembered body so that he could experience a resurrection. Because of her devotion in gathering the pieces and reassembling them, Isis became the indirect savior of all mankind, while at the same time giving to Egyptian women the knowledge and belief that they too shared in this special mission. For Egyptian women womanhood was more than a role. It was a glory and a devotion.

In addition to the belief in the history and theology of Isis, was the confession that it was woman who had been the giver and maintainer of the Nile which was seen as a woman whose large breasts overflowed annually so that her spiritual children, the mortals who ringed her waters, would have refreshment and new growth. To this end the sexual movements of the woman, except for menstruation, were accorded a healing property.

It is true that on occasion Egyptian woman shared her honor and place with other women in the larger harems, especially those of pharaoh, but these were exceptions rather than the rule. The harem was established more for political reason than for dynastic or sexual reasons since the pharaoh, if male, traditionally wed his sister and had his children by her so as not to bastardize the blood line. This is most dramatically testified to by Ramses III who openly envied the majority of his subjects who had only one wife to contend with, acknowledging that a harem bred intrique and assassination plots.

If life with a husband was difficult Egyptian women had open access to the courts who would deal with marital discord. The courts recognized her as the undisputed ruler of the household. She was also the legal owner of the family furniture and other possessions.

If there was any attempt to deprive the Egyptian woman of her status in the home, or to take away her possessions, she could sue for the restoration of either or both. With few exceptions she won her case.

If she was divorced by her husband, regardless if she was the first wife or one of the "minor" wives, she was with few and rare exceptions granted a generous alimony. Furthermore, she could contest a divorce action litigated by her husband, or she could countersue or initiate the original suit. She had little difficulty in winning her case when she demonstrated the ill-treatment she may have received at the hands of her husband for wife beating was never permitted nor sanctioned. All that was required of her was to show the judge her bruised breasts and arms and the case was decided in her favor. If she did not wish to obtain a divorce, but sought to have her

husband "corrected", should could request that he
be fined or publicly whipped. The judge listened.
To return to the woman's favor, if the husband
sought to keep her, he frequently composed love
poems as he had done in his courtship days. She
determined their merit, and unless they noticably
touched her emotionally, she did not take him
back, for marriage was to be lasting and gracious,
not brutal and haphazard.

Once a woman reached the age of eight, nine,
or ten, she was considered to be of marriag-
able age. (Even queens, such as Cleopatra, married early by contemporary standards, for their lon-
gevity was short.) A marriage contract was drawn
up between the two families which were to be united through the marriage of their children, and it
was notarized. Eventhough the document was reg-
istered the marriage was not considered to be binding until after the first year that the couple
lived together.
The first year of marriage was considered
critical for both the man and the woman. Known as
the "year of eating" the first year was strictly
probationary for both parties. It was during this
time that the couple experienced the fullness of
one another, to learn whether or not they could enjoy and appreciate the other's uniqueness and separate personality: especially the eating habits
(and sounds) of the other. It was commonly held
that if a couple could tolerate the eating habits
of each other the marriage would endure.
It was also during this "year of eating"
that the man was to test the culinary habits and
expertise of his wife. The woman was expected to
discover if she was capable of expanding the man's
eating pleasures and increase his interest in new
foods.
If the "year of eating" prove abortive the
couple were released from their contract. The

money payment was returned and each went his/her
separate way. However, if the situation seemed
tolerable they renewed their committment in a
public ceremony and celebration and became "as
one."

If children were born to this marriage, they
were welcomed and maintained in a near
nursery atmosphere.

The joy of giving birth to a new family
member was spectacular. Frequently the entire family gathered to watch. It did not matter if the
child were a boy or girl, for each was given suck
and attention. Frequently the mother nursed the
child until it was entering puberty, as testified
in the reliefs at Thebes carved during the Twenty-
sixth Dynasty. However, once the child was considered to be capable of being independent of constant supervision (usually at the age of four or
five), to took its place in the family as an near-
equal partner: tilling the soil, creating bricks,
blending and mixing grains, baking bread, and the
like. The child did so with little need to be asked, for the child traditionally was taught to not
only obey but become directly involved without having to be asked. To this end those children who
became a contributing member of the family found
public and personal praise, as defined and exhibit-
ed in the various tomb inscriptions which carried
the central message: "I was one who was loved by
his father, praised by his mother, and loved by
his brothers and sisters for I obeyed the laws of
my family."

When the family laws were broken, punishment
was swift and sure. Beatings were frequently administered by priests who carried the authority of
the god/dess, and who firmly confessed the maxim
"a boy's ears are his backside." Girls, too, experienced this "learning", but her trials were
less frequent and the punishment tended to be more
gentle, unless she "became uncorrected and required a new application of learning."

The majority of the nonpunitive education

for women was in the area of domesticity. Formal
academic education remained closed to women for
centuries. When it was opened to Egyptian women
it was in the area of religion and literature:
many becoming officiants or poetesses.

The extent of the woman's contribution to
literature is still unknown since much of Egyptian
literature remains untranslated from the original
hieroglyphic compositions. Still records do exist
detailing academic toils and triumphs which led to
moments of abandonment to wrestle, swim, fish and
hunt. Occasionaly the capable scholar (or obed-
ient daughter) was indulged with a tournament
where the expertise of a select coterie was demonstrated to parents, kindred, and sometimes an entire community, although most tournaments which
featured girls were confined to the home, or on
special intimate family outings, as in the case
of the Pharaoh Nakht who frequently took his children with him on fishing expeditions. The royal records show his daughters in close and constant attention. The eldest stands behind him, while her
younger sister crouches down and clasps her
father's calf. Other works show them participating in the catch. One girl hits the water with
sticks, while the other poses with (either a real
or an imaginary) spear about to throw it at a passing fish.

Hunting was also popular, but it was enjoyed
more by men and boys, than by women and girls. E-
ven then both sexes used the domesticated dog in
the quest. So popular was the dog that it was created a god, and given this dog-god, known as **Abu-
bis** for its own protection.

Anubis was one of the oldest and most reverr-
ed gods of ancient Egypt. Countless shrines were
built to this fascinating deity, and several holidays were called in its name.

Because of Anubis, and the general love for
dogs, dogs were found everywhere, and in the city
of Cynopolis, dogs were even mummified in belief
that they would attend their doting owners in the

next world. The only animal that equalled (and at time surpassed) the dog was the cat. This animals was especially prized by women, and was universally given a place of importance in every Egyptian home.

So prized was the cat that women alone cared for it since women were considered more careful than men in treasuring the life of the earth, and were the first to domesticate it. It is with little doubt that one can safely argue that women even gave it its name: **miw** which reflects not only its nature and sound, but its relationship to the spirit.

To give additional companionship, women also domesticated monkeys, baboons, and various birds which roamed the home freely, frequently settling at the feet of the women as they labored preparing meals or arranging the household possessions.

ONE OF THE TWO HOUSES FOR WOMEN BELONGING TO 'EY

Baking, cooking, cleaning, all were necessary, but they were not the only occupations of
women who remained at home. Women were also expected to create, master, and enjoy games they
could teach and challenge their family with. The
most simple games required only motor skills, and
included such activities as running, jumping, and
playing a game similar to leap-frog, where the participants leaped over those who were crouched down
with their head between their legs. Balls also appeared, and later dolls became a passion for young
girls, who were addicted to "tending its needs":
feeding, dressing, and washing the dolls who were
fashioned as nearly lifelike as the artist and art-
isan was capable. Doll clothes were even made by
mothers, and among the most affluent the wardrope
of the doll frequently equalled their own in number and quality.

Adult women spent countless hours playing a
game similar to chess. **Draught,** or Egyptian
chess was such a popular sport that special tables
were specifically designed for it, and when the
enthusiasm for the game grew so intense the table
and the chess pieces were taken outside and placed
under a large tree. Draught tournaments were
especially popular, with the play being conducted
by a throw of the dice in order to control the
moves of the black and white pieces over a board
of thirty squares.

There were religious overtones to the game.
Many Egyptians were convinced that the agil
draught player would win the favor of the deities
who would be quick to help him/her in times of ad-
versity. This helps explain why modern archaeolog-
ists have found so many draught sets inside the
early tombs.

Women also enjoyed dancing. Dancing was
especially popular during celebrations and religious festivals.

In most cases Egyptian dancers were nude. So important was the dance choreography that the spectators wished to miss nothing of the movement of the artists.

The majority of the dancers were young girls. They pranced, shimmied, and shook their bead collars to make them rattle. When they became exhausted they fell freely to the floor or on a couch nearby to watch another group (usually of adult women) perform acrobatics until their strength revived and they were able to return to the center of the floor.

The music to which both groups performed was orchestrated by both men and women. The music itself was generated by strings, woodwinds, and brass instruments. The main instrument was a five foot harp crusted with gold; it took its tone from a highly decorated sounding box on which it stood.

The harpist sat cross-legged on the ground to stablizze the sounding box. Stratling the instrument the musician played with poise. She was accompanied by a lead female lute player and several less prominent male lutests, who enjoyed a monopoly over the long single flute, while women played a small double pipe flute which enjoyed an ivory mouthpiece.

The entire orchestra was blessed with an especially strong rhythm section. This section was composed of clappers, drums, and tambourines, as well as a special instrument called a **sistra** which was a small hand held metal instrument surmounted by the head of a cow from whose horns wires ran, and on which metal discs were threaded so that when the instrument was gently shaken it produced a rather pleasant sound, or if it was harshly shaken, it brought a clashing and blaring sound quite unpleasant to hear. (In addition to the **sistra** being used to orchestrate the dance, it had two further uses: one to drive away evil spirits, when gently shaken, and, the other to assist the woman in childlabor, when harshly shaken.) Many of these instruments were found in the

House of 'Ey where women were given special apartments where each chamber was devoted to a distinct
and exclusive use, without male interferrence.

In comparison to the rest of the world at
that time, Egypt and Egyptian women were remarked-
ly different. The Greek historian, Herodotus,
gives us the most colorful account of life and the
role of women in Egyptian society, in his famous
History:

As the Egyptians have a climate perculiar
to themselves, and their river is different in its
nature from all other rivers, so have they made
all their customs and laws of a kind contrary for
the most part to those of other men. Among them,
the women buy and sell [while] the men stay at
home and weave; and, whereas in weaving all others
push the woof up, the Egyptians push it down.

Men carry burdens on their heads. Women
[carry burdens] on their shoulders.

Women urinate standing. Men [urinate]
sitting. They relieve nature indoors, and eat out
of doors in the streets, explaining that things
which are unseemly should be done in private,
while things which do not offend should be done in
the open.

No woman is dedicated to the service of any
god or goddess. Men are dedicated to all deities:
male or female.

Sons are not compelled to support their
parents against their will, but daughters must do
so, even if they are unwilling.[34]

Αἰγύπτιοι ἅμα τῷ οὐρανῷ τῷ κατὰ σφέας ἐόντι
ἑτεροίῳ καὶ τῷ ποταμῷ φύσιν ἀλλοίην παρεχο-
μένῳ ἢ οἱ ἄλλοι ποταμοί, τὰ πολλὰ πάντα ἔμπαλιν
τοῖσι ἄλλοισι ἀνθρώποισι ἐστήσαντο ἤθεά τε καὶ
νόμους· ἐν τοῖσι αἱ μὲν γυναῖκες ἀγοράζουσι καὶ
καπηλεύουσι, οἱ δὲ ἄνδρες κατ' οἴκους ἐόντες
ὑφαίνουσι· ὑφαίνουσι δὲ οἱ μὲν ἄλλοι ἄνω τὴν
κρόκην ὠθέοντες, Αἰγύπτιοι δὲ κάτω. τὰ ἄχθεα
οἱ μὲν ἄνδρες ἐπὶ τῶν κεφαλέων φορέουσι, αἱ δὲ

γυναῖκες ἐπὶ τῶν ὤμων. οὐρέουσι αἰ μὲν γυναῖκες
ὀρθαί, οἱ δὲ ἄνδρες κατήμενοι. εὐμαρείῃ χρέωνται
ἐν τοῖσι οἴκοισι, ἐσθίουσι δὲ ἔξω ἐν τῇσι ὁδοῖσι
ἐπιλέγοντες ὡς τὰ μὲν αἰσχρὰ ἀναγκαῖα δὲ ἐν ἀπο-
κρύφῳ ἐστὶ ποιέειν χρεόν, τὰ δὲ μὴ αἰσχρὰ ἀνα-
φανδόν. ἱρᾶται γυνὴ μὲν οὐδεμία οὔτε ἔρσενος
θεοῦ οὔτε θηλέης, ἄνδρες δὲ πάντων τε καὶ πα-
σεων. τρέφειν τοὺς τοκέας τοῖσι μὲν παισὶ οὐδεμία ἀνάγκη μὴ βουλομένοισι, τῇσι δὲ θυγατράσι
πᾶσα ἀνάγκη καὶ μὴ βουλομένῃσι.

Even in the area of transportation and
public life Egypt was different from other societies. Herodotus continues, noting that both men
and women share the same boat when traveling down
the Nile. And, whereas women in other societies
remain quiet and passive during a boat journey
(and give the men the best seat if men should hap-
pen to be with them), Egyptian women were exactly
opposite: they were the entertainment. They made
noise with rattles and flutes while singing, en-
couraging others to join them in song. Men reluct-
antly agree, and finally the entire entourage
breaks into harmony. Their enthusiam celebrated
in song does not abate until the boat reaches its
destination.

Even as the boat docks, the differences between social tradition remains acute. While in
other societies the men take over the docking of
the boat, in Egyptian society both sexes help
shore the boat, and then together disembark.[35]

Most boat excursions were to holy shrines.
Those who took sail went either as religious pil-
grims or penitents. Yet the penitential system of
ancient Egypt was anything but remorseful; in
fact, it was quite gay.

Religious observances (save for the mourning
of the passing of pharaoh) were festive. A great
deal of wine was consumed, and games were enjoyed.

The most somber occasion was the internment

of the dead. Egyptians were quite concerned with the passing of souls from earth, and built a strong and viable theology around it.

While Egyptians of the Old Kingdom gave only limited attention to the belief in life after death (according it proto-Calvinistic properties: being limited to a select royal few, such as pharaoh and royal counsellors, who entered a boat steered by the sun-god Ra, who sailed to the eastern most part of the sky) they laid the seeds to a more complex theology of death. Once the dead arrived at a strange garden-like eternity, they met with Maat, the goddess of Truth. Coming before her, the goddess would take the heart of the departed and place it into a large dish on one side of a scale. On the other pan she would place a magical feather. Once this ritual was performed she would call in the dog-headed god Anubis, who would adjust the balance.

While Anubis was adjusting the balance, the ibis-headed god Thoth entered to record the verdict on a roll of papyrus. Then the trial began.

A jury of forty-two Assessors (one for each of the sins that could disqualify the dead) entered and watched. If the heart and the magical feather balanced one another exactly, the dead was allowed to enter into the Eternity of Delights, guided by the god Horus who led him/her into the presence of Osiris. But, if the heart was heavier than the feather, the Devourer appeared within a twinkling of a star.

The Devourer was frightening to behold. He had a head of a crocodile, the forefront of a lion, and the hindquarters of a hippopatamus. He would catch up the damned, crunch the dead's bones, and then munch on his/her flesh while drinking noisily of the cadaver's blood. (Although this concept of heaven and hell may seem strange and frightening, it must be remembered that at this same time no other major nation had developed any concept similar in scope or importance. In fact, ancient Israel still denied the existence of both heaven and hell, as the Psalmist wrote: **The dead do not praise you, O Lord, neither all they that go down in silence.**)

Later the Egyptian concept of heaven and hell was somewhat softened. The dead were no longer to be judged only by the insight of a magical feather, but their eternity was charted on the basis of how s/he lived and died, with greater pains taken to determine the extent of charity given, respect shown, and laws obeyed.

Since the concept of heaven and hell softened with the advance of Egyptian civilization, so too were there changes in the popular attitude towards death and dying. Whereas little preparation was made for the internment of the dead in general during the Old Kingdom, greater care was taken to preserve the cadaver in the Middle and New Kingdom. Much of this advanced because of the increased definition of death and the soul which was divided into four different parts.

The most important souls of the individual were the **Ka** (or primary soul), and the **Ba** (or secondary soul) which wandered abroad and could select any shape it chose. The third soul was the **Akh** which was the soul that went to the next-world to be damned or admitted to all the delights of eternity. The fourth, and final soul was the **Sekhem** which was nearly identical to the **Ka**.

It was each individual's personal responsibility, and the responsibility of his/her heirs to take all necessary measures and precautions to provide for the **Ka**. To this end elaborate tombs were built, and into these tombs wonderful and exotic gifts were stored: including a wide range of furniture, boats, **objets d'art**, jugs of wines and containers of grains. Sometimes, as was the case with the entombment of Queen Nitocris, subjects were also buried, either after they had died or even while they still were living: sometimes these subjects included the immediate family and kindred of the deceased who believed that by so dying they too would earn eternal peace and pleasure.[36]

Women had a special place in the theology and history of the dead. They were not only equal to men, but considered essential to be with men if men were to ascend to the judgement with little difficulty. Furthermore, the gods seemed to take an extra special interest in the women when they appeared at judgement. Seldom were they devoured, usually they went on into the garden there to join the vivacious convivialities awaiting them. Men were not always so lucky.

Funeral Stele of Lady Nofert
In this grave carving from the mid-third millenium, found at Giza, the wife of a leading nobleman sits before an offering stand containing loaves of bread. Lowie Museum of Anthropology, University of California, Berkeley

the Minoans

There exists few records today that give an authentic picture of ancient Minoa. Much of contemporary belief concerning this ancient civilization comes from Plutarch, which current archaeological discoveries is proving to be incorrect. The tales, fables, and oral histories passed down for generations is now being rejected.

Current research and investigation, especially that of Yannis Sakellarakis and Efi Sapouna-Sakellaraki, is changing our concepts of Minoan civilization.[37] Their finds show us that Plutarch's argument that Minoa was a peaceful, pastoral society is unrealistic and unhistorical. Gentleness and graciousness, good government, and astute economics were not practiced in Minoa.

Instead the Sakellarakis discovery points to a quite different picture. Ancient Minoa was at best a primitive and barbaric society which practiced, at least in part at special times, human sacrifice.

Part of the theology of ancient Minoa which colored its civilization and social concept came from its geographic location. Situated on the Island of Crete in the middle of the Mediterranean Sea, Minoan civilization experienced severe earthquakes which savagely ripped apart her homes and treasuries at least thirty-seven centuries ago. For this reason the people turned to their religious leaders to supplicate the gods to remove the curse of the tremors.

The religious leaders were both men and women. While current evidence points to the male role as being dominate in the religious exercises, especially to the actual sacrifice of young boys, women too took an active role in the ritual. She carried the vase that held the human blood of the victim. She was, furthermore, responsible for presenting it to the gods in libation in the same manner as animal blood was poured upon the sacred rock/altar/soil to appease the divine wrath.

Bare-breasted, with her skirts tightly bound at the waist, this priestess tied up her hair and adorned it with ringlets of gold rope. Gold charms fashioned into snakes coiled around her arms, and sometimes rings adorned her toes.

There are numerous representations of women in ancient Minoan civilization. She was regarded as the source of all life, and thus countless mother figures were carved out of stone and wood. These figures were set in temple/houses which could be found in nearly every dwelling place and business.

Nearly all of the mother figures were fertility images: ranging from arms seductively beseeching the faithful to enter, to blossomed wombs rich and ripe with the fruit of future nations. If men appear with them they are usually to be found on top of the structures, looking down into the temple from a hole in the ceiling. Such temple structures and holy images were sold on a lavish scale, some even going with the dead to their graves, as was the case at Phourni, where the mother-figure sometimes was joined by a daughter figure representing regeneration and rebirth or reincarnation.

Additional to these temple figures detailing the image of women, we are fortunate to have tooled signet rings and other jewelry which lavishly depict women and their place in society. In some cases they are represented as women bull-jumpers: stripped to the waiste with their dress trussed around their abdomen, they are shown grabbing the horns of a bull in order to hurdle over its back in open competition with men. In other instances the women are foresters and lumberwomen: planting saplings, or uprooting bare-handed sacred trees to be used in kindling the holy fires in preparation for sacrifices of sacred bulls or young men. In other scenes they are shown as collectors (tax, goods, and offerings) which they carry to the common Treasury. And finally, they are seen on ships, and in nautical businesses, participating on par with men.

Home life and domesticity was also important but the records are unclear as to the extent of the role of either sex in the home. What we do know is that women and men in ancient Minoa enjoyed color, space planning of furniture, and accessorization of shelves, tables, and other pieces of furniture. Red was the most popular color with gold and yellow following. This was especially true in the ornamentation of jugs for grains, oils, and wine, as well as other pottery.

Women and men in ancient Minoa were especially fond of pottery that was as thin as egg shells. These were decorated with scenes from every day life, and became a mark of her own success for they recorded specific incidents rather than a definite fixed motif.

The ancient Minoan home also boasted of decorated walls. The most common wall ornament was the double-headed axe which were sometimes made from pure gold. Those that were hammered out of pure gold were of an obvious religious nature and not used in war, for they have not been dulled by blood or carnage.

Evidence points to the high probability of women in ancient Minoa also taking an active role in warfare. They are pictured fighting as Amazons in a variety of battles; however, their forte remained in commerce, especially in the dealings of Minoa with Athens and other Greek states.

In commercial adventures women appear to be responsible for seeing that inventory was kept under control, and that accounts were maintained. If accounts became past due it was not uncommon to seek some method of collecting on them. War was a simple solution, but it proved costly and more was lost than gained. To circumvent this the Minoans required hostages for the debt incurred, and if the debt was not paid the hostages were either sold into slavery to pay for the debt, slain, or more commonly sent to the arena to serve as sport for the viewing of Minoans who enjoyed watching the inexperienced attempt to hurdle bulls, escape bears, and avoid other wild animals. Few foreign slaves were kept for fear that they might escape and make their way into the common Treasury. To protect the Treasury wild, mad bulls were chained to the central entrance to gore those who approached. It is quite possible that all of this was the foundation for the famous legend of Theseus and the Minotaur.

The extent and importance of the Minoan treasury can be seen in the legend of King Minos, who to this day is equated with unusual wealth. News of this massive wealth intoxicated many foreign adventurers, until finally around the year 1600 B.C., Minoa was successfully invaded by the Mycenaeans, routed, and enslaved.

The coming of the Mycenaeans put assunder the basic equality of women on the island. They, like their Dorian counterparts, held women in low esteem, and soon confined them to the isolation of the **gyneceum**.

With the advent of the Age of the Greeks, women were not only shut off from social intercourse and competition with men, but also restricted and confined in clothing, hairstyling, home determination, child rearing, economics, and politics. Their hair was required to be long, their breasts were covered, their activities limited to gossiping and giving birth to children whose very life and destiny was strictly in the hands of the man. They were forbidden to speak in public, and unless they were temple priestesses, they seldom were allowed to activiely participate in religious exercises.

More than anything else the Dorian Greeks are responsible for settling the current western psychology against the equality of women. The advances of the ancient past, especially in areas of Egypt and Minoa, and Etrusca, were shunned and put away.

Endnotes

1.   Xenophon, Anabis 1.5.1; cf. Leonard Woolley, **The Ur of the Chaldees** (1950); Samuel N, Kramer, **History Begins at Sumer** (1959); Edward Chiera, **They Wrote on Clay** (1938); and, James Mellaart, **The Earliest Civilizations of the Near East** (1964).

2.   **Code of Hammurabi** 128.

3.   Ibid., 129.

4.   Ibid., 132.

5.   Ibid., 175.

6.   Ibid., 142.

7.   Ibid., 143.

8.   Ibid., 141.

9.   Ibid., 148.

10. Ibid., 143.

11. Ibid., 190-194f.

12. Ibid., 195.

13. S.N. Kramer, **The Sumerians** (1964) p. 251.

14. **Code of Hammurabi**, 109.

15. Ibid., 110.

16. Ibid..

17. Ibid., 145.

18. Ibid., 152.

19. Ibid., 151.

20. Ibid..

21. H.W.F. Saggs, **The Greatness That Was Babylon** (1962). Popular accounts include, C.W. Ceram, **Gods, Graves and Scholars** (1951), and James Wellard, **By the Waters of Babylon** (1951).

22. H.L. Mencken, **A Mencken Chrestomathy** (1949), p. 67f; W.K. Loftus, **Travels and Researches in Chaldaea and Susiana** (1857), p. 163f.

23. J.B. Pritchard, **Ancient Near Eastern Texts** (1969), p. 67.

24. **Ibid..**, p. 590.

25. **Ibid..**

26. Kramer, **op. cit.**, p. 150.

27. **Ibid..**

28. Psalm 137.

29. Herodotus, **History**, Book VII, 99.

30. **Ibid.**, Book VIII, 93.

31. **Ibid.**, 68-70.

32. **Ibid.**, Book II, 14.

33. Quoted in A.H. Gardiner, "Ramesside Textes Relating to Taxation and Transport of Corn," in **Journal of Egyptian Archaeology** 27 (1941) 19-20. See also, George Steindorff and Keith C. Steele, **When Egypt Ruled the East**

(1942), dated, but reliable and easy reading.

34.   Herodotus, **loc. cit.**, 35.

35.   **Ibid.**, 60.

'Ες μέν νυν Βούβαστιν πόλιν ἐπεὰν κομί-
ζωνται, ποιεῦσι τοιάδε. πλέουσί τε γὰρ δὴ ἅμα
ἄνδρες γυναιξὶ καὶ πολλόν τι πλῆθος ἑκατέρων ἐν
ἑκάστῃ βάρι· αἱ μὲν τινὲς τῶν γυναικῶν κρόταλα
ἔχουσαι κροταλίζουσι, οἱ δὲ αὐλέουσι κατὰ πάντα
τὸν πλόον, αἱ δὲ λοιπαὶ γυναῖκες καὶ ἄνδρες
ἀείδουσι καὶ τὰς χεῖρας κροτέουσι. ἐπεὰν δὲ πλέ-
οντες κατά τινα πόλιν ἄλλην γένωνται, ἐγχρίμ-
ψαντες τὴν βᾶριν τῇ γῇ ποιεῦσι τοιάδε· αἱ μὲν
τινὲς τῶν γυναικῶν ποιεῦσι τά περ εἴρηκα, αἱ δὲ
τωθάζουσι βοῶσαι τὰς ἐν τῇ πόλι ταύτῃ γυναῖκας,
αἱ δὲ ὀρχέονται, αἱ δὲ ἀνασύρονται ἀνιστάμεναι.
ταῦτα παρὰ πᾶσαν πόλιν παραποταμίην ποιεῦσι·
ἐπεὰν δὲ ἀπίκωνται ἐς τὴν Βούβαστιν, ὀρτάζουσι
μεγάλας ἀνάγοντες θυσίας, καὶ οἶνος ἀμπέλινος
ἀναισιμοῦται πλέων ἐν τῇ ὀρτῇ ταύτῃ ἢ ἐν τῷ
ἅπαντι ἐνιαυτῷ τῷ ἐπιλοίπῳ. συμφοιτῶσι δέ,
ὅ τι ἀνὴρ καὶ γυνή ἐστι πλὴν παιδίων, καὶ ἐς
ἑβδομήκοντα μυριάδας, ὡς οἱ ἐπιχώριοι λέγουσι.

36.   In order to avenge her brother who had
been a pharaoh of Egypt, and who was slain by his
subjects, Nitocris determined to execute those who
were responsible.   Building a large underground
chamber, she announced plans for a large feast,
and invited those who were implicated in the assassination.   Her guests eagerly came, and while
they were feasting she opened a secret lock of the
river and flooded the underground chamber.   Although she later was universally praised for her
act of filial piety, she feared vengeance and so
threw herself into a fire she had built.   See, Herodotus, **loc. cit.**, 100-101.

37.   Yannis Sakellarakis and Efi Sapouna-
Sakellaraki, "Drama of Death in a Minoan Temple,"
in **National Geographic** 159.2 (1981) 205ff.